# BROKEN PIECES
and the Lessons Learned

3G Publishing, Inc.
3600 Park Lake Lane
Norcross, Georgia 30092
www.3gpublishinginc.com
Phone: 1-888-442-9637

©2013 Keith Pellerin. All rights reserved.

No part of this book may be reproduced, stored in a retrieval system, or transmitted by any means without the written permission of the author.

First published by 3G Publishing, Inc. February, 2013

ISBN: 978-0-9833544-5-1

Printed in the United States of America

Because of the dynamic nature of the Internet, any web addresses or links contained in this book may have changed since publication and may no longer be valid. The views expressed in this work are solely those of the author and do not necessarily reflect the views of the publisher, and the publisher hereby disclaims any responsibility for them.

Keith Pellerin can be contacted at keith.pellerin@gmail.com.

## *Foreword*

A while back, I had an interest in serving the poor and hurting. Shortly after praying about this, I met the author, my husband Keith, who introduced me to an outreach ministry to help the poor and homeless. The circumstances in which we met gave validity to the writings in this book. The fact that he reached out to me was a living example for me, of the things written in this book. Together as a team we would go out on Saturdays to Atlanta to visit the poor and we would hand out food and minister to the homeless and the downtrodden. I can tell by the experiences he has shared with me and with others, that he has a heart for the hurting and broken. God has used him to reach out and change lives with his testimony; he still visits the park where God has changed lives through him. He has helped people without homes and placed them in shelters and he has even brought some people into his own home. He has encouraged hurting people who are lost or have walked away from God, not to give up hope and now their lives have been changed and placed back in a right relationship with God.

In society there are many people who are hurting. There are people from all walks of life who come from broken homes where children are being abused by parents, where there are victims of spousal abuse, children raised without a father in the home, divorce and families affected by drugs and violence. It is amazing to know that God can use the tragedies of life which many think are meaningless to bring about healing and restoration in the lives of many others. With all the technology in the world today most people have lost touch with the reality that we serve the same God who continues to intervene in the lives of people, especially those who desire to have a relationship with The God of The Bible. This is the same God who worked miracles in the lives of many, from biblical times to the present day. The same God, who parted the Red Sea, opened blinded eyes, healed the sick, and cast out demons. This book tells the stories of how God intervened in Keith's life and how God desires to intervene in your life as well. It shows how God can take the mess we have made of our lives and turn it around for our good and the good of those around us.

My husband Keith, who has a personal relationship with God, believes that you too can have a personal relationship with the Creator of the universe. Give your heart to Him, He will never fail you; He can take your tragedies and turn them into triumph. From Keith's childhood to his adolescent life, he has experienced hurt and rejection through various circumstances and this story is about how God used those experiences to reach out to those who are hurt and broken.

This book talks about experience after experience with God and illustrates that by being obedient to God, having a willing heart to follow Him regardless of the cost, God can use you to do great things. My husband has a heart to follow God. Following God is not easy like many proclaim, if so everyone would. The Word of God says, in Matthew 7:13-14 "Enter through the narrow gate. For wide is the gate and broad is the road that leads to destruction, and many enter through it. But small is the gate and narrow the road that leads to life and only a few find it". There are many tests and trials mentioned in this book that helped Keith to better understand what other people go through before he was able to have a better understanding of life. Many people give up hope or lose their direction; or believe they have made too many mistakes for God to use them as instruments of His love. This book shows us that it's not God that gives up on us, but we give up on Him. This book shows the reality that God will never leave nor forsake us.

I am reaching out to you, the hurting, helpless, and broken to let you know that God can meet you where you are and restore you. You can be helpful in the Kingdom of God when you reach out to other hurting people. My husband's life has been broken and restored. He has heard the voice of God and has accepted the challenge to reach out and help those who are also hurting and broken and restore them back to meaningful lives with direction and purpose.

I encourage you as you read this book that God will take the BROKEN PIECES of your life and use it to do great things in the Kingdom of God.

Tamara R Pellerin, Wife

## *Contents*

| | |
|---|---|
| FOREWORD | iii |
| INTRODUCTION | ix |
| CHAPTER ONE<br>*In the Beginning* | 13 |
| CHAPTER TWO<br>*Strongholds* | 19 |
| CHAPTER THREE<br>*Sticks and Stones* | 25 |
| CHAPTER FOUR<br>*Valuable Lessons* | 31 |
| CHAPTER FIVE<br>*A Father's Wisdom* | 37 |
| CHAPTER SIX<br>*God's Way is Higher than Our Ways* | 43 |
| CHAPTER SEVEN<br>*Enemies Now Friends* | 53 |
| CHAPTER EIGHT<br>*Tempted & Tried* | 59 |
| CHAPTER NINE<br>*Filled* | 65 |

| | |
|---|---:|
| **CHAPTER TEN**<br>*Lead By The Spirit* | 71 |
| **CHAPTER ELEVEN**<br>*Dreams and Broken Dreams* | 77 |
| **CHAPTER TWELVE**<br>*Bold Steps of Faith* | 85 |
| **CHAPTER THIRTEEN**<br>*Blinded by Sin* | 91 |
| **CHAPTER FOURTEEN**<br>*Another Trip Around the Mountain* | 99 |
| **CHAPTER FIFTEEN**<br>*Refreshing Others* | 109 |
| **CHAPTER SIXTEEN**<br>*New Beginning* | 117 |
| **CONCLUSION** | 125 |

## Introduction

The way I am going to share my story, which is my testimony, is by taking you on a similar journey. I want to share all the lessons I have learned from all of my Broken Pieces, specifically those lessons which are deeply rooted in God's word. God has brought me through so many trials and errors and refined me by using the broken pieces as literal teachings and truths that have shaped me into the man of God I am today. As I walk you through, highlighting Gods divine intervention in my life, it is my prayer and hope that you will understand the lessons that I have learned in my experiences, and be able to see the importance of God in your life. So as I tell my story, I will share the ups and downs, the miracles and wonders, the joys, pains and sorrows, but most importantly the Glory of God and his infinite wisdom, and how He could use a pitiful soul like me to advance the Kingdom and spread His gospel. Like Jesus and his parables, I hope to share with you these lessons learned in hopes that you will seek Him, love Him and worship Him for who He is and what He has done. In the name of Jesus, it is my prayer that you will allow the Holy Spirit to impart knowledge and wisdom in your heart to live a righteous and pleasing life unto the Lord. This is my story, based on truth, based on God's grace and mercy, His promises and His word, and my response to His love.

This is a story that would not have been written unless the hand of God was not upon me. I could not have made up something like this if I wanted too. If I could, I never would have. I would have never chosen this path in a million years. Like you, I would not have taken some of the paths our lives lead us to, if I would have known before-hand where I was going. The things I am writing are all true to the best of my memory. It is the story of the life of a believer in ***Jesus Christ***, who has been shown great mercy. It is my hope that my story gives hope to the hopeless and courage to keep going despite what you feel or see. Things seem less complicated when you are reading the story, but when you are living out the reality, *that's another story*! Some parts most likely, never would have been written if we had a say in it. I am sure Joseph would not have opened his mouth about his dream had he known it would have landed him in a pit, had him sold into slavery, put into a prison, lied about, lied to and caused all the other heartaches he went through. I am certain David, a man after God's own heart would not have chosen his path either had he known that to be anointed King would lead him to stay in caves for ten years and hunted down like an animal, have his family ripped to pieces-*had he known all that*, he probably would have said "Thanks, but no thanks. I do not need a crown, it's not worth all the trouble"… but by the same token he would not have affected the countless number of lives through the centuries had his story been told any other way. I am in no way trying to compare my life to these two great Men of God. No way! I am only making the point that you or I would not have drawn up the plans for our lives (*and the way our lives turned out*) if we had been able to choose the final outcome of our life. Scriptures says that "a man chooses his way but God directs his path." (Proverbs 16: 9)

Before I start sharing my journey with God with you, I would like to explain the point I am trying to make and the message I am trying to relay within my story. The first thing is very basic. **Jesus loves you**. For God so loved the world He gave his only begotten son and while we were yet sinners he died for us. There are plenty of scriptures about giving, but you may say what about the verse that says the Lord gives and the Lord taketh away. I believe the very act of taking away, is an act of love. When our loving Father removes something or someone from our lives, the motive of His heart is Love! God is love and every good parent is going to give his children good gifts and remove from their lives those things which are harmful to them either physically or spiritually. The only thing is that we do not know what good really consist of. The word of God says we call good evil and what is evil, good. For example, we may say "that the women I slept with last night (who happens not to be my wife) was good" but the word of God calls it fornication which God says is evil. Men call the act good because of the pleasure involved in the act, but God calls it evil because there is no commitment to one another and children will have to live with the shame of their parents and having no order in the home. We may say it is bad to live by these rules, the Ten Commandments, and that God wants to just take our freedom. But God said it is good for us to live by His word and His commandments.

The law of the Lord is perfect, reviving the soul (Psalms 19:7). While we are talking about the goodness of God, I would like to say this while it is fresh on my mind and I'll try to bring this out as I share my story. The word of God says He loves the just and the unjust. Have you ever done something for someone and they never thanked you or even acknowledged it? God shows His goodness to mankind all their lives even if they never recognize it. That is love. That is grace. God never changes. He always loves though we never respond to it. We on the other hand, if someone does not show some kind of thanks for the smallest thing we do for them, we are ready to sign their death certificate, put them in the grave and remember them no more. "Bless God there is nobody that is going to treat me like that. Who do they think they are? I am the son, daughter of a king." No, that is the very reason they are treating you like that…"the servant is not greater than the master, if they treated me this way. They will also treat you this way because you belong to me," so sayeth the Lord.

# CHAPTER ONE
## *In the Beginning*

I would like to share with you my personal testimony in this chapter. I won't use real names or names of people involved in my life, as I do not want to cause offense or any unnecessary harm to anyone. The reason I named this book Broken Pieces is because I believe it portrays my life, and I believe this is what God put on my heart to name it. This is a story of how God takes the broken pieces of our lives and uses it to be a piece of someone else's life. God does not waste the things we suffer in, if we allow him to use it to help others.

I grew up in a small town in Morgan City, Louisiana. I was one of seven children. I was the one in the middle. I have three sisters and three brothers. We lived a pretty normal life, middle class, we were not rich and we were not poor. My dad worked for the phone company, Bell South. My mother never worked, that is not for any company, but worked full-time raising seven children. If you have any children you know that is a lot of work. I'm not for certain, but my mother said I was the crybaby of the bunch, always wanting her attention. You have to get what you can when there are six others to compete with.

The first memory I have was wrecking into a fence on my bike. This was the first sign I remember that life hurts. I was real small and haven't grown much since. Our neighbor had several girls, no boys. So, I guess I had my first girlfriend at five years old. I remember when I first went to school, I was only five years old and some kid tried to pick a fight with me. I still remember this like it was yesterday. I had on a yellow shirt and this kid grabbed me by the shirt and tore one of my buttons off. I was glad that was the only thing that was torn off. Then to make things worse my neighbor, a little girl I liked, was in my class and she took up for me--- how humiliating was that on my first day. This was the beginning of my low self-esteem.

I don't really remember anything else that sticks out, until I went to elementary school. I remember first starting to like sports and girls when I was in about the sixth grade. I also remember getting into my first fight. One of the kids, who was supposed to be "Mr. Bad", picked a fight with me. I don't remember what it was about, I only remember fighting and he never did get a punch on me, but neither did I get a shot on him. He walked away and the other kids laughed at him, and called him a chicken. So, I walked away feeling pretty good. That was my first touch of the mercy of God, because as I walked away, he called me back to fight again because the other kids were laughing at him, but I just kept walking leaving well enough alone. Later we became friends, I wasn't the kind of kid that picked on people, but I wouldn't back down if they came my way, even though I was small for my age.

I remember waiting to get old enough to go hunting with my dad. My older brother was hunting with dad and some of my dad's friends. I wanted my dad to be proud of me, but by the time I got old enough to go hunting, they quit going. This really bothered me, but I just pushed it down and buried it. As you know when you push it down eventually it has to come up and out somewhere. I think this is when I began to build up some anger inside. I remember losing my temper one day at home, I don't remember what about, but I do remember pitching a fit about something. I never forgot this because for whatever the reason, it sticks out to me. My mother had said to me, "You are always angry like a little banty rooster." That's a fighting chicken, if you don't know. I remember this so clear, and how I felt. I was maybe 10 or 12 years old and I thought to myself *"I'm dying on the inside, and you're too blind to see it."* Back then, I blamed my mother because I felt she didn't care. As I grew older, especially when I had my own children, I realized it wasn't that she didn't care, it was just she was so busy raising seven

## In the Beginning

kids and never had a break. As a child I didn't see my mother's side, I only saw my own side and that was I wanted to feel loved and care for by my mother. This is why so many children act up at home, school, wherever. They want to be noticed, appreciated and loved. If they don't find it at home they will go looking elsewhere. Some will find it in gangs, sex, drugs, and drinking, looking for love in all the wrong places. Sometimes children are loved, they just don't perceive that they are loved and that was my case. I didn't see it, at least not the way I wanted it anyway. I went to church as a child, but I never had a real understanding of God or faith or love, etc. I don't remember having any deep discussion about God with my parents. If we don't have a strong foundation of faith, when life hurts come our way (and they surely will), Satan will give us many ways to cope with pain. Unfortunately they are all destructive to your life, because they only take away the pain temporarily. We can run to our destruction with open arms. The word of God says that Satan comes to blind our eyes to the truth. When we get involved in sinful habits to medicate our pain, we become more blinded by the day. This is when Satan begins building strongholds in your mind. A strong hold is a mind set or thoughts in your mind that don't agree with the word of God. For example, someone tells you no one really loves you, your ugly, or it could be something that seems positive like "your smarter than your friends" or better looking and it causes you to become either too proud of who you are, or have a negative outlook about yourself. Either one is wrong, because it's not based on truth. Our worth is based on the fact that God loves us, not someone's opinion. Only God's opinion matters. The only problem is most people don't know God, or that He loves them, so they settle for other things trying to fill that deep hole inside of them.

We were created to be loved by God and to love God in return. No other love will satisfy that vacuum of not having God on the throne of your heart. There are certain things we use in life that help us along the way. For example, like bleach to get something clean, but we all know bleach can destroy material if you use too much of it. In a similar fashion God created things in life for us to enjoy, but if we use them out of order, or too much, in other words if we let them become an idol to us, it will destroy us. For those who may not know, an idol can be anything we put before God, or we replace God with. The word of God says, "God is a jealous God", He won't allow anything to compete with Him for your love. (Deuteronomy 6:15/Exodus 20:5)

Many people's lives are full of idols and they don't even know it. Whatever you love will show by what you do with your time. If you love sports you will spend your time playing sports or watching sports. If you love the arts you will spend your time at museums. If you love God you will spend time in His presence, talking to Him, praying, and worshipping him. Whatever captures your mind and your time has your heart. We can do all the talking we want about loving God, but if our actions don't equal our words, it's only talk, nothing more. If you tell your wife how much you love her, but you're always in the woods hunting or fishing, she knows it's only talk, and you know the old saying, "talk is cheap"…. how you spend your time tells the real story. I am not saying it is wrong to go hunting or fishing, but it shouldn't be more important than your wife and especially, your God.

# LESSON ONE
## *Fellowship*

I was sadly reminded of this aspect of our relationship with God today. I received a phone call from someone asking if I could help them, not "how are you doing today "or "I have missed talking to you." However, I went to pick up this person and I helped them out. Then when I got home, lying on my bed, God spoke to me. He said "that's the only time people speak to me too." Isn't it amazing how everything we have comes from God yet the only time we speak to Him is when we need something? If you did a survey of how much time you spend in fellowship with God, it probably would not take much paper. This is really sad, but true. How many parents of children in nursing homes are dying of loneliness because their children have no fellowship with them?

## In the Beginning

Some parents have sacrificed their entire life for their children and yet they never receive a visit from their children. This is a downright shame especially for the body of Christ. These people aren't dying of health problems, their dying because no one cares. Therefore, if you have loved ones or friends who are all alone, take time and invest in their lives. It could be the difference between life and death. How much more does God deserve for us to spend time with Him? God will never be more or less of whom He is without our fellowship, but we will; yet the fact remains God desires to have fellowship with us.

I could read all the books in the world about someone and yet still never really know them. Someone I once worked with comes to my mind immediately. She came up to me one day at work and said, "You know when you first started working here, I couldn't stand you." I thought, "Oh that's nice to know", but then she said, "That was before I got to know you. Now I see you completely different. You are not at all how I perceived you to be." Then she told me that my life was affecting a lot of people I worked with, which was good news to me because at the time it seemed like most of my efforts were in vain. Let this be an encouragement to you when you're pouring out your life for others and it seems like you're wasting your time. You are not, even if people never show they're grateful for your kindness. The God who sees you in secret will reward you openly so do not grow weary. (Matthew 6:4)

Then there is another aspect of fellowship that I would like to mention. It is found in 1st John, Chapter 1:6. "If we say we have fellowship with Him, and walk in darkness, we lie and do not the truth." I hear so many people say, how they have a good relationship with God, but never obey Him. The only one we are fooling is ourselves. That would be like your wife coming up to you and saying, *"Hi honey, I just slept with your best friend and stole all the money out of your wallet"*, and thinking she would be fine with it. I do not think so, but yet that is what we do to God daily, and still think all is well. Give me a break! People never stop and think God has feelings too, and we can grieve Him in that way too. Does God quit loving us? *No*, but this limits or destroys our fellowship with Him. The word of God says to have no fellowship with darkness. I hear people say Jesus hung out with all the sinners, so I can do the same. Yes, He did, but His motive was completely different. He loved them into the kingdom; He did not take part in their sin, major difference. You can say all that hog wash you want, God knows the real intent of your heart. That is where the rubber meets the road, as they say. If you want to play games with your salvation or eternity that is your call, but I would not advise it as it is not very smart. In Psalms 15:1-5 it reads, "Lord, who may dwell in your sanctuary? Who may live on your holy hill? He whose walk is blameless and he who does what is righteous, who speaks the truth from his heart and has no slander on his tongue, who does his neighbor no wrong and cast no slur on his fellowman, who despises a vile man but honor those who fear the Lord, who keeps his oath even when it hurts, who lends his money without usury and does not accept a bribe against the innocent. He who does these things will never be shaken." You can't get much clearer than that. You can't live on both sides of the fence, so make sure you're in the right yard.

# CHAPTER TWO
*Strongholds*

The next thing I remember was going from elementary school to junior high school. This was a big change for me, because I went from being in an all white school to a 60 or 70 percent black school. I didn't have a problem with race, but I didn't know if they or race had a problem with me. I remember feeling afraid of how I would be accepted. Things went alright as far as race was concerned and before long I fit right in, even learned a few new words, some of which I can't repeat. This is when I first started learning about sports. I had never really played much before that time, so naturally I was pathetic. I would be the last one picked when teams were selected. Dad had played sports in high school and was a pretty good athlete. You couldn't tell I was his son by the way I played, I stunk. I didn't realize it at the time that the ability to play was always there, but I had just never tapped into it.

By the time I got to high school I was just as good, if not better than the kids in my class at sports. This is what I felt important doing, so I spent all my time playing sports and lifting weights, trying to win the approval of my father, even though he was unaware of it, and to a great extent so was I at that time. I remember playing my younger brother in a game of ping-pong, I started losing, and he started laughing at me. I threw the paddle at him as hard as I could. If I would have hit him, he would be playing ping-pong with Jesus. Back then, winning meant everything to me. I made winning the focal point of my life because I wanted others to recognize me for my abilities and strengths. If I won, I felt loved, if I lost, I felt worthless. That's really why winning was so important to me. Winning was life, losing was death.

# BROKEN PIECES

This is where Satan really tried to build this stronghold in my mind which is what I was talking about earlier. At the time, I was completely unaware that he was doing this to my life. Satan does his best work in the dark. He had erected a castle in my mind and the foundation as always, was built on lies that my worth was in winning. Winning was my idol and at the same time God was also working in my life, and I was also completely unaware of His existence in my life.

There were several times in my life where I attempted, by winning, to get the approval of my father. Even though I played as well as the other kids, for some strange reason I would always miss out on what I wanted. I remember entering this contest to see who could throw the ball the farthest and I lost by a foot. Then I went out for the baseball team my brother played on. During tryouts I couldn't have played any better, yet it was as though as an unseen hand always held me back from getting what I wanted: to win and to be accepted by my father. Like I said before, my father knew nothing about how I was feeling. I wanted his approval by doing well in sports. These thoughts consumed my mind, even though my father did nothing to make me feel this way. I know now where my thoughts were coming from. Satan wanted me and now he wants you to feel worthless by having us try and make attempts to be accepted for various reasons, all of which are based on lies. You have great worth because of who you belong to (God), not what you accomplish or fail at in life. Your value is based on the fact that Christ died for you. How much more value do we need? In order to know this, we must have a personal relationship with Jesus. We MUST believe with our hearts, and not doubt our value.

The word of God says it didn't benefit Israel because what they knew wasn't mixed with faith. You must believe that, your life depends on it, whether you realize it or not. You may say at this point, "Well I don't have any faith." This is not true; the word of God says He's given everyone a measure of faith. You may not have much, but you do have some. The way to begin is to use the little that you have. How do we get more faith? Well God's word says faith comes by hearing, and hearing by the word of God. It also says faith works through love. If your faith isn't working, check your love tank, and see if you're running on fumes. Also, this hearing is not only hearing with sound, but obeying. The word of God talks about not being hearers only, but being doers of the word. What that means is that when you hear the word of God and disobey it, you are automatically deceived. Lack of love and disobedience is the real reason we have little or no faith. Also a lack of knowledge plays a part in this as well. My people perish because of lack of knowledge, check your bible.

It is also based on truth. The word of God says we can't believe just anything; it must be founded on truth. The following is an example of someone believing something not based on truth. This was mean on my part, I still don't know to this day why or how I let this guy do this. I had a friend that I hung around with when I was a teenager…actually he was my brother's friend. Anyway, there was a box in my yard turned upside down, it was a small box. This friend bet me he could kick this box over the fence, which was only about 10 or 15 yards away. He had faith or believed he could, I knew he couldn't because my knowledge was based on a truth and I knew something he didn't know. Well he put his hands up like he was going to kick a field goal, then he kicked it as hard as he could, but it didn't budge. He didn't know that there was a car battery under that box. He could have broken his foot, and probably still has nightmares *and a smaller shoe size on one foot.* He went on and on about how cruel I was and being the sensitive person I was, the more he complained the harder my friends and I laughed. With friends like us, who needed enemies? I realize now, how dumb that was on my part, but back then it was hilarious. He is probably still having flashbacks and telling his children about the time his low life friend tricked him into kicking a car battery. My dad still laughs about that now, 30 years later. The point I am trying to make is, our faith must be based on God's word not something we dreamed up or something we want. God's word promises to answer our prayers according to His will, this should be the foundation of our entire prayer request. For example, God's word promises us He will supply all of our needs according to His riches and glory.

# BROKEN PIECES

Therefore, we have a foundation of truth on which we can base our faith. If God's word promised it, we shouldn't be worried where our next meal is coming from. If we are not getting our needs met we need to check our hearts. The problem is on our side of the fence, not God's side. I would like to stop here to make a point before I move on, getting back to where I kept falling short of getting what I wanted, winning and my father's approval. I remember being very angry at God even though I knew little or nothing about God. Somehow in my mind I got the idea that the reason I wasn't getting what I wanted was all God's fault. I remember yelling at God, "You just want to take everything from me…go-ahead take everything I don't care anymore." I was dead serious about it too. I wasn't even sure there was a God, but if there was, it was all His fault.

Looking back now, I can see how I grieved the Spirit of God. I guess that's one of the things Jesus had on His mind when he was dying on the cross, when he said, "Father forgive them for they know not what they do'" I was wrong, but I really didn't know what was going on, I just knew someone was to blame, and I blamed God. In time, I realized that God not allowing me to have the things I wanted was His protective love. He turned my attention from the things of the world to the things above. Years later, my children accused me of not caring, when I had the most pure intentions possible. It was then I realized how wounded the heart of God must have been when I accused Him of not caring for me, when all the time He was protecting me from eternal destruction. My children have ripped my heart out when they accused me of impure motives, but I can say with all honesty, I understand. I can say with Jesus, "Father forgive them for they know not what they do." That is how we get true understanding, we walk in their shoes. Whether you are the parent or the child, don't look to blame; just cry out to God for understanding. It will save you a lot of unnecessary pain, both for yourself and others.

## LESSON TWO
### *Chastisement*

Chastisement means to punish, to scold sharply. (Merriam-Webster)Sometimes when you see someone punished or when it is you being punished, it seems cruel and unnecessary to some degree. The first thing we should remember is God has infinite knowledge of every situation in your life, and also in everyone else's life. The second thing is even when we are being punished severely we should try to remember God never acts out of character or emotion. All His decisions are based on one thing and one thing only, love. I do not know or do I claim to know the reasons, but what I do know is it is based on love. Have you ever made a bad decision, or acted in a rebellious way, and been chastised? Then you wanted to blame God for not stopping you from doing the dumb thing you chose to freely do?-- I have. All the pouting and complaining will only make things worse. I've gotten so many stripes; my rear looked like a zebra. The best thing you can do when you're being chastised is accept it and thank God for it, because as long as you keep a rebellious attitude it will only get worse. Remember when David took a census in 2 Samuel Chapter 24:15? "So the Lord sent a pestilence upon Israel from the morning even to the time appointed, and there died of the people even from Dan, even to Beersheba, seventy-thousand men."

Seventy-thousand peopled died because of David's disobedience. Do I understand that? No I do not, but I'm not God and neither are you. So what are we to do when we can't understand the Lord's chastisement, complain, murmur, and turn away from God? Where will you go, who will you turn to? There is only one answer, at least only one that makes any sense. That is back to God. Sometimes our rebellion has far more consequence than we realize. So think long and hard before you disobey God. Your life is tied to so many others, both good and bad. In Psalms

118:18, it says that "the Lord has chastised me sorely, but has not given me over to death." Chastisement is actually mercy, but it just does not feel like mercy. Whatever we receive as chastisement would be far worst for our lives and the lives of others, if God would just let it go.

We will never know the evils that have been prevented because of God's chastising. Look back over your life and see had you not been corrected what would have happened that could have totally destroyed your life or the lives around you. The Word of God says He chastises those he loves. Those not being corrected are illegitimate. The worst kind of judgment from God is to be not chastised. Even though at the time, it does not feel so great. However, the results will be great for your life and everyone involved. Do not think you are being kind to your children when you let them get away with murder (figuratively, not literally). One day you will be sorry, so protect your children with a good rear end adjustment. It goes a long way. They might not like it now, but one day they will thank you. Even if they never do, you'll have peace, knowing you have done what was for their best. If they have any sense they will, and so you should be thankful to God. That is the best antidote for chastisement. Be thankful, it will definitely be in your best interest. Remember God always loves you though you may never understand it until we stand before His awesome presence. To God be the glory!!

# CHAPTER THREE
*Sticks and Stones*

Now my junior high school years were over. I was now preparing to go to high school, whether I felt ready or not. Maybe the reason they call it high school is because at this age and sometimes even before, literally everyone starts getting high. This was not the case with me, for whatever reason, it was the grace of God I never had a desire to use illegal drugs and I never have buckled to the desire even as an adult. Many so-called friends tried over and over to try and get me to do drugs, but I never would. It was not that I had a great value system in place back then, I just had no desire at all. I thank God I didn't because I have seen and known some of the people I grew up with who totally destroyed their lives with drugs. High school wasn't fun for me, for the most part. I couldn't wait to finish and had no desire to go to college. I hung around with some of the less popular jocks at school. My parents should have named me Casper because I was like a ghost at school. I pretty much was completely unknown. I did pretty good as far as my grades. I graduated 10$^{th}$ in my class, but there were only about 90 students that graduated in my class.

I remember one time we had a new girl come to our school from another state and she was very pretty. We were all sitting in the gym at recess and someone was introducing her to everyone. As I mentioned earlier, I was like a ghost, they introduced her to everyone, except me. I felt about as worthless as anyone could feel. I didn't say anything, but that really hurt. Then, on another occasion, two of my so-called friends told me that this new girl liked me. I was feeling pretty good about that, so I decided to go and sit next to her in the gym. The gym was packed, and when she noticed I was sitting next to her she got up and walked off. That was bad enough, but it gets worse. I was so embarrassed I got up and started walking out of the gym behind her. She thought I was following her, which I wasn't. I only wanted to leave and go find something to crawl under. In any event, she started screaming in front of the whole school. I wanted to go to fall asleep and never wake up. I hope that you are now starting to see the big picture here…why I wasn't such a great fan of school.

I believe I had one girlfriend the whole time I was in high school and that didn't last for very long. Although I did have a few good friends, High school wasn't a very good time in my life…in fact I was pretty miserable most of the time. I hid a lot of pain by laughing or joking a lot. The people I hung around with thought I was pretty funny. I made them laugh, but I was crying on the inside. I also had a very dirty, potty mouth, which was another way of hiding the pain inside. All these things continued to build self-hatred on the inside, though I really didn't realize it at the time. I believed what I saw, and what I saw was that people were cruel and no one cared. Therefore, I came to the conclusion that I was worthless.

So many people struggle with low-self esteem, even people that you think have no reason to feel this way, but they do. I have known people and known of people who were some of the most popular kids in school, such as star athletes who ended their lives. I wish people would really think before they say the cruel things they say and do to others. An ugly comment can take root inside an individual on the receiving end, and it can completely destroy their life. You know the old saying sticks and stone will break my bones but words will never hurt me? Words may not hurt you physically, but they kill you on the inside. The word of God says there is life and death in the tongue. Therefore, we need to take care of what we allow to come out of our mouths. For our own sake and for the sake of others, please think before you speak. Remember, God said we will be held accountable for every idle word we speak, God have mercy on us all.

I know people that cannot forget the hurtful things that

were said to them. They live in a prison, trapped inside of themselves, being held captive by someone's sharp tongue. If you are one of these people, give your pain to God and forgive the ones who have hurt and wounded you. When you forgive them, God will heal your pain and set you free. It's a process so don't get down and out if it takes a minute. The choice to forgive is an act of your will, but the wounds heal a little at a time. There are cases where people have been healed instantly, so trust God to do what is best for you.

Most parents do not have a clue of what their children go through at school. If you have children in school, let me encourage you to talk to your children and give them the freedom to tell you how they feel, not what they should feel. You will be surprised by how much pressure there is on your child to measure up to the other popular students, to do things they don't really want to do. As a parent and a protector, they need you to listen. It will go a long way, it may save their lives, it's that important.

I met a young couple at the park one day. It looked like they were living in their car. I walked up to them and asked if they were alright. The young man told me they had been married for about a year and the following week they would have a place to stay. I started sharing the gospel with them. As I began talking to them, I couldn't help but notice the pain and despair in the eyes if this man's wife. It was heart wrenching just to look at her. She was so wounded she couldn't even look at me. She was sad and held her head down the whole time. I asked the young man if I could pray for her and he was open to that. He said he would walk away while I prayed for her. He had also told me she experienced a great deal of abuse while growing up, which for me was painfully obvious. Her disposition (or appearance) was that of a sad, broken, and hopeless spirit. I could sense that this young woman had most-likely experienced both physical and mental abuse and even verbal abuse. There was shame, possibly even guilt. I couldn't help but think about how many times she may have been made to feel worthless, unimportant, and insignificant by the mindless, cruel words of someone. This is the point I have been trying to make about the power of life and death in the words we speak (the

# BROKEN PIECES

tongue). Someone's words had this young lady so wounded, it was unbelievable. We need to reach out to those hurting to let these people know someone cares. We have to pray for our young people, its life and death. It could be your child out there.

## LESSON THREE
### *Formed*

This means to take shape, to mold or shape to conceive in the mind. In Genesis 1:1-3 It states, "In the beginning God created the heaven and the earth, and the earth was without form and void, and darkness was upon the face of the waters, and God said, let there be light, and there was light, and God saw the light that it was good and God divided the light from the darkness." If you look at creation you will notice how God forms different things from one way to another. For example, a baby is formed in the womb of his mother. A diamond is formed in the earth. A pearl is formed in the sea. If you looked at them in the beginning stages, you wouldn't see anything that looked like it would amount to very much. Look at the finished product. Two seeds become a living breathing child, an old worthless piece of coal becomes a diamond, out of a slimy oyster, and we get a beautiful pearl. At one time, there was little worth, but when completely formed great value is born. In the same way, God takes our lives, puts His Spirit in them; little by little we are formed into His image. God supplies all we need, we supply our free will. If you say, "Yes, God I give you the freedom to act in my life," your willingness to allow God to form you into His image is the most important thing you will do in life, not to mention one of the most painful. It is also the most fulfilling, and peaceful. I know the two don't seem to mix, but they do.

Once we crucify our flesh, our spirit rejoices. Many people are not willing to pay the price, but unfortunately, they pay the ultimate price, separation from God. To whatever degree you allow God to form in you His image, to that degree you will share in His power and glory. You will also share in his joy and peace. If God allowed painful circumstance in your life, even though you caused it by your bad choices, you can believe there is a reason for it. He's forming the instrument that He desires to use. Why did Jesus become a man because He thought it would be a fun thing to do, not hardly. One reason is so He could identify with us. If you're talking to someone about your problems or a situation in your life, you want someone who has been there and done that. The hurts in life form a big hole inside of us.

When God heals us of our deep hurts, we are able to pour out of the river that God has placed in our heart. For instance, don't come try and tell me how to trust God when I'm struggling with the desire for sex or loneliness, when you have a woman next to you in bed every night. It may be right what you're saying, that I should trust God, but if the person telling me that has never gone through what I'm dealing with they can't really know or understand to any heart level what I feel unless they have lived through it themselves. When you have gone through, and come out on the other side, I'm more willing to listen. I can pour out into your life what God has poured into mine.

The word of God says "not to be conformed, but transformed by the renewing of your mind." (Romans 12:2) We must put the word of God in our heart. If we don't, Satan will put his words in your mind and heart. Then instead of being formed into the image of God, we will be formed into the image of Satan. Don't you see people who don't serve God? They have the same attitude as Satan himself. Most people don't see themselves in the light of God's word. One young man told me if God would have told him not to eat that apple, he would not have been so stupid to eat it, as Adam and Eve did. I said, "You eat it every day and don't realize it. The word of God says don't fornicate, lie, cheat, steal, etc., but you do it all the time." It is the same thing Adam and Eve did, disobeyed God. They disobeyed God's word. One lady told me something she had done that she thought that the word taught. I don't remember what it was she said, but it wasn't against what the word taught. Then I told her it wasn't wrong and she was glad, but then I told her because she *thought* it was wrong and *still* disobeyed, it's all the same to God… it's *still* disobedience because she violated her conscience. God judges the intent of the heart, not just the actions.

Whenever you're going through difficult circumstance, don't drive yourself insane trying to figure it out. Just know God will use it for not only your good, but also the good of others. I'm not saying we shouldn't try to understand what God's doing, but if you don't understand don't blow up your brain trying to figure it out. Be at peace and trust God. Trust God with all your heart and lean not onto your own understanding. God may give you understanding about it, but if He doesn't, be at peace and trust God. There are things in life we will never know, keep moving, spend your life obeying the things you do understand, not trying to figure out the things you don't--- your life will be much better off if you do that. Did it help Job when he tried to figure out what God was doing? The only thing it helped was having a nervous breakdown. Job came to the conclusion that basically he knew nothing and repented for thinking he did, once God revealed himself to Job. The longer I live, I realize the less I really know. Let God be God.

Another important part of being formed is in Galatians 4:19. "My little children for whom I am again suffering birth pangs until Christ is completely and permanently formed within you." We must pray that Christ is not only formed in us, but in the people we are praying and suffering for. For Christ to be formed in you, you must and will face opposition and suffering as it is part of our identity with Christ. Remember He was a suffering servant acquainted with grief. In addition, Satan is forming a weapon against you, trying to destroy your life and the influence you have with people. The word of God says no weapon formed against you will prosper, but there will be a weapon used, and it won't prevail. Keep praying and don't stop until you're in the grave, because Satan won't quit until your last breath. So, be strong in the power of his might. Amen!

# CHAPTER FOUR
## *Valuable Lessons*

Well, I am out of high school now and moving on. Once I finished school I just wanted to get a job and get married. Getting married and having children was something I wanted more than anything, but before you get married, it would help if you had a girlfriend, right? There was one girl that I dated just as I started my senior year. I got a call from this young lady who attended a school nearby. She also went to the same church I attended. She was one of the most popular girls in the school, so I had to wonder why she was calling *me*; I did not exist at my school. She asked me to go to the prom. I thought it was another nasty joke being played on me. When she called she said "Hi this is Cindy" (which was not her real name), "would you like to go to our prom with me?" I said "you want to go with me?" I could not believe it, but she really wanted to go! We did go but it did not turn out like I wanted it to. We had a couple of dates after that, and then she went off to college. I guess it was not meant to be. If nothing else, it made me feel a little better about myself.

I learned a valuable lesson, that sometimes we don't always see things the way they really are. Sometimes we are our own worst enemy and we need to pay close attention to how we view ourselves and others. We need God's help to accomplish that. He sometimes shows us a part of us, through other people. Don't believe everything you think or feel, good or bad. Ask God to show you who you are…He knows all.

Soon after she went to college, I landed my first job at a Winn-Dixie grocery store. I can't remember the manager's name, but I think it was Mr. Lucifer, or his twin brother…..at least that is how he treated his employees. This man definitely should have read a book or two on how to win friends and influence people. He was constantly cutting people down and nothing was ever good enough. Do you know anyone like that? Not the kind of company you like to keep… hopefully, you are not that person. If we do have to say something to correct someone, let's make sure we do it in love. Getting back to the story, I had the opportunity to transfer to a different store. It wasn't a hard decision for me to make. Things were much different with my new store manager. He was kind and taught me what to do and made me feel good about the work I was doing. This made all the difference in the world. How we treat people has a lot to do with the response we get in return. This new manager thought I was the best thing since sliced bread. I worked my way into a full time position with one catch.…..they wanted me to go back to the store and work with Lucifer again. (I really can't remember his name!) Now Lucifer knew I would never work for him again, but he was wrong. I took the job and God honored this. This manager treated me different this time around. You see, God is still in the business of changing hearts, even the most hardened ones. Sometimes he will use your life to do just that.

Later on they asked me if I would take the position of assistant manager of that same store. I declined the offer because I knew once I accepted, I could be transferred all over the country and that was not in my plans. I didn't want to move. During this period of my life, my eyes were opened to how deceitful and judgmental people can be. One example of this was another assistant manager that worked in the same store, but a different department. He told me I was a "smart a___."; you know the animal Jesus rode in to town on….some of you will get it! But once he started working with me and got to know me, he told me I was the only person he liked in the whole store. This just goes to show you that we shouldn't be so quick to judge. Things aren't always what they seem to be, good or bad. For instance, like the manager who was so kind to me, wasn't so kind to his wife. He invited me to a strip club with the intention of cheating on his wife. Even though my relationship with God was not that strong, I had no desire to be a part of that. I don't know what became of him, but this I do know.…if his life

## Valuable Lessons

choices didn't change, it wasn't good. God's plan for our life is good, but Satan also has a plan for your life...to kill, steal and destroy everything in your life. Be careful who your friends are, you may become like them.

About the same time was when I got my first car. It was a 1970 Plymouth Fury. They named it right as it made me furious because everything that could have gone wrong and broke--- did. It was the first car to ever die of cancer, but before it died, I traded it in on a Cutlass Supreme. This was one of my favorite cars I ever owned. I had some loud pipes installed on it. Then my brother's friend (the one that kicked the battery) got one just like mine... only difference was the color and the fact his father paid for it. I had to work for mine. Sadly, just like he wrecked his foot, he wrecked his car. He was dating a young girl and tried to put his arm around her and kiss her, but instead he kissed the mail box on the side of the road. Some guys got all the breaks...just so happened, all his were bad breaks. The reason I am bringing up the cars is because this was one of the lessons you never want to forget. A few years later I had bought a brand new Trans Am and about 8 months later, I found out it had some serious problems. I let my brother talk me into trading it in on a brand new Toyota Celica. The problem was that my brother did not want me to tell the people where I was trading it in that it was about to blow up. My gut told me to tell them the truth, but my brother told me that was not necessary. Well, I listened to my brother and you know how it took God six days to create the earth, it took six days to destroy the new car I just brought and on the seventh day, God rested. Yes, six days later I completely totaled my car. When my Dad saw it going down the street pulled behind the wrecker he thought I was dead by the looks of my car, but I did not even have a scratch.

I learned another valuable lesson. Listen to your heart and do not try and deceive someone. That was the last time I ever tried to cheat someone. I got the point the first trip around the mountain. God had tried to warn me, He told me not to do that. Sometimes God speaks like Fred on the old sitcom Sanford and Son, because after I decided to listen to my brother instead of God, he said

# BROKEN PIECES

'YOU BIG DUMMY"! I hope that this may save someone some unnecessary pain and trouble. Listen carefully to your spirit when God is speaking to you. It could have cost me my life and if not for the mercy of God, it would have. I had another unpleasant lesson with cars. I had the need for speed. I remember telling one of my friends, "I speed all the time, but I never get caught"… and right after I made this bold proclamation, Yes you guessed it! *"Bad Boys, Bad Boys going get you!"* I got about 3 or 4 tickets for speeding and reckless driving in about two weeks. My car insurance was like the national deficit. "Pride comes before a fall." Proverbs 16:18.

The word of God says if you are going to boast, boast about Him! I learned to keep my mouth shut at least for a little while. For the most part, we never learn unless we pay the price. Some learn by the warning of others, but not many. When I got all of those tickets it caused my foot to lose a few pounds and perhaps saved me from killing myself or someone else. Most times when we suffer some loss we only see the negative side of it, the negative side being the tickets and the positive side protecting me from killing myself.

## LESSON FOUR
### *Integrity*

Integrity is defined as strict compliance to an ethical standard, the state of being whole or sound. (Merriam-Webster). In Psalms 25:21, it states "let integrity and uprightness preserve me; for I wait on thee." Yes, it says it will preserve me. The fact you do what is right from the heart will save you from many pitfalls, and troubles. Just in the natural not even counting your relationship with God, it preserves you. What happens when your wife, your children or friends find out you have been lying, cheating and deceiving them? There goes your marriage, your friends and possibly your life. It just makes good sense to have integrity of heart. Once you lie to someone, you lose the trust factor between you and the other person. I have seen and experienced how just one lie can poison the best of relationships. I worked at a huge manufacturing plant at one

## Valuable Lessons

time. I overheard a coworker talking to a fellow employee. He told this employee to come and ask me something, because he knew I had a reputation for telling the truth. What do your friends and associates think of you? Can they trust you? If they do, are you going to disappoint them?

God wants us to be people who can be trusted. What if God was like us, one day he says he loves you, the next day he does not. Would we ask people to be satisfied with that type of fickleness? Yet we go through our lives living like this on a daily basis, calling it little lies, white lies, no matter what color it is, it's all the same to God, lies and deception! In Him, there is no darkness. I brought my car to a mechanic to get it serviced, to get my timing belt changed. His mistake caused my timing to jump, which means I needed a new motor. The mechanic wanted me to pay for the parts that he messed up, and he would cover the labor, does that sound like a good deal? I paid for what he broke. I paid for the parts, but never went back. I made sure no one else I knew went to him either. Was I paying back evil for evil, no just protecting someone else from being taken advantage of? These same people, when things fall apart in their life will find some way to blame God. You ever had someone tell you if you ever need help just call me, then when you take them up on it, they don't answer the phone. Then they wonder why the people they try to get to come to church do not show up. I will tell you why, they are looking at your life.

I have heard many people say you just cannot make it if you are honest. Haven't you heard nice people finish last? That is great news, because Jesus said the first will be last and the last will be first. Whose words are you going to believe, men or God? Put the shoe on the other foot, would you want other people telling you some of the whoppers (lies) you've been telling. In this case, you will be eating the whoppers you made. This is an order that you don't want to place in your life (dishonesty). If people realized what they deal out will be dealt back to them, they would think twice about being dishonest. God's vision is 20-20, He can see you, and the ones that *can't* see are us. The people who seemingly get away with things, in my opinion and I believe God's also, are the worst off, because in most cases they have all of eternity to regret what they themselves have done. God have mercy on us.

Come on people, let's live with integrity, not only for your sake, but for everyone involved. Someone's soul may depend on it. What if a person never comes to God because of our lack of integrity? I know we are not fully responsible for other people's actions, but we will have to give an account. Jesus said scandal will come, but woe to whom through it comes, it would be better that he had a millstone tied around his neck and thrown into the bottom of the sea. Not a place of destiny if you know what I mean. If you have been unfortunate to lead someone astray and are truly repentant then God has enough mercy to go around. I know I've needed several rounds and will continue to need His mercy the rest of my life, and so will you. So let's honor God by being people of integrity. Everyone will benefit from it especially you. If the people of God were people of integrity, there would be so much growth in the church it would be unreal.

# CHAPTER FIVE
## *A Father's Wisdom*

About this time in my life, I was pretty unhappy, actually miserable. I said to myself there has got to be more to life than this. That is when I began to learn more about God. I started searching on my own, not because someone was forcing me, but because God had been working in my life, and for the most part I was unaware of it. I had a lot of doubts about whether God even existed. I believed He did, but had many doubts. This is also the time Satan started working overtime in my life. He does not mind working extra hours if he thinks he can wipe you and your future out. That is his goal and you know he is very good at it. He's had thousands of years of practice and he has perfected his craft, yet I hear so many people saying how dumb the devil is and calling the devil names... *that is pure stupidity on our part.* First of all, in Zechariah 3:2 the word of God says not to do it. When Satan came against one of the most powerful angels, Michael the Arc Angel, he only said "The Lord rebuke you." God does not only give us authority to rebuke the Devil, he says to "resist him and he will flee." God's word gives strong warnings about cursing at the Devil and those in authority; we would be wise to heed the warning. This is found in the book of Jude chapter 1: 9-10. "Yet Michael the Arc Angel when contending with the devil about the body of Moses he did not bring against him a railing accusation, but said, "The Lord rebuke you. But these speak evil of these things which they know not but what they know naturally as brute beast in those things they corrupt themselves." If you continue to read the rest of that chapter the words are stronger. Take the warning and do not speak about things you know nothing about.

# BROKEN PIECES

During this time in my life, I wanted to get married and have children. Sometimes what *we* want and what God wants are two different things or we're not willing to wait for God's timing. We allow weaknesses in our heart to overthrow what God is trying to do in our hearts. Guess what happens when you try to over throw God, let me give you a guess… pain. The very pain we are trying to avoid is increased by not doing things God's way. I had started dating this young lady. I think I was about 19 years old and this was one of those times I allowed my weakness or desire for something to get me in trouble.

My dad tried to warn me about this particular young lady, but you know how it is when you are 19 years old, you know more than everyone. My Dad told me I would be going out the front door to work and she would have someone coming into the back door. I was so blind because it was something I desperately wanted. I lost my virginity and opened my life up to a lot of pain doing it my way. I found out my Dad was right. One of my friends had previously dated this girl and I was now engaged to her. He told me she was still calling him. I did not believe him either. However, he proved it to me by letting me listen in on a phone call from her. She was playing the game on me. I was devastated. That was the end of the relationship.

Instead of being thankful to my Dad, I was angry at him. I somehow believed my Dad just did not want me to be happy. I showed him contempt instead. How we hurt the people we love the most when we want our way. I now realize we do the exact same to God. He is trying to protect us and we are totally blind to His love because we desire something other than Him. I am on the other side of the fence now and my own children acted just like I did. How I grieved the heart of God, yet He continues to love me.

This painful process taught me something about the heart of God. Yes, I get angry with my children when they disobey me, but it is more for their sake than mine. I only want the best for them. This is what I would like to say to parents, look at your children

## A Father's Wisdom

from a different point of view, God's view. It will save you and your children much less misunderstanding and heartache. Your children want the same thing you want and what we all want is to be loved and accepted. I am not saying not to correct them, but do so with more compassion and understanding. It will go a long way and will reach into eternity…right to the heart of God. Not long after that relationship was over, I got into another bad relationship. I am going to explain this a little more than I would like, not to glorify sin, but to show how God was being merciful to me even when I was sinning against Him.

In my case this was more of weakness than not trying to do what was right. Like I said before, God was beginning to convict me of my own sin, but it was a great struggle for me, wanting to do what is right and wanting my way at the same time. Well, here goes…. This girl was doing everything in her power to try and get me in bed with her, even though I was talking to her about God and trying to do what was right. She convinced me to do it her way. Therefore, I agreed to take her to one of my friend's house and give into her desires. On the way to pick her up, this song came on the radio called "Stairway to Heaven." I was on my stairway to Hell. My conscious was really screaming at me, *Do not do this*, but I put cotton in my ears, so to speak, and kept riding. I picked her up and went to my friend's house. I let her get completely undressed, but I just could not go through with it. I told her to get dressed and I took her home. She was so mad she could not stand it. That was the end of that. Then two weeks later, I saw her brother and he told me she was pregnant.

Now, I saw why God was screaming so loud at me. He saved me from marrying *Run Around Sue*, which is a song, not her name of course. If you are not old like me, you may not actually know that is the name of a song. I would have married her thinking it was my child. Walking away from that was a big miracle like parting the Red Sea, because this girl was beautiful. Satan knows just what to use to destroy you. If it were not for the mercy of God; that is exactly what would have happened. Try and remember when things are not going according to your plan, that it was not

God's plan. His plan is for you to prosper as your soul prospers. It is more important to God that character is built into your spirit than your temporary pleasure.

# LESSON FIVE
## *The Mercy of God*

This is something very near and dear to my heart. I cannot say this without tears because I have received an abundance of His mercy and continue to receive it every moment of my life. Mercy triumphs over judgment. As I look back over my life, I see the mercy of our great God too many times to count. His mercy endures forever. Mercy is not taught, it has to be experienced. I heard a story of a pastor visiting a jail. I have been there, and it is not a fun place; sorry for getting off subject, I cannot help myself-- *anyway to the story of the quest.* An (Inmate) asked, "Hey preacher, why don't God give us what we deserve?" The pastor said, "If God gave you what you deserved the floor would open under your feet and you would fall into hell." Maybe not the answer he was looking for, but one he needed to hear! "There is none good, not one." We have all gone astray no not one righteous, (Romans 3: 10-12). Mercy is not being punished when we should be. Have you ever done something you should not have done and not been punished for it? If the answer is no, I just have one thing to say to you, "Liar, Liar your pants are on fire!" If that does not make the picture clear, I have another one for you… "All liars will be in a lake of fire." Let us move on. I think you got the point. The truth is we all have …and I have done more than my share; *I'm not bragging*, just stating the facts. Let me ask you a question, what would other people say if asked the question, "Is (insert your name) merciful?" What is your answer about yourself? I know people do not always have a clear understanding of things especially when it concerns them personally. Do yourself a favor and think about all the times people have done you wrong or you believe they have done you wrong. Sometimes we think people have done us wrong because we, or our way of thinking may be incorrect, distorted…

maybe even twisted. Think of all the times you have done wrong to others and how God was merciful to you. Look real good based on the Word of God, *not* your goofy perceptions. Now, are you merciful to the people who have hurt you? Just remember "the measure by which you measure out will be measured back unto you," (Matthew 7:2). This possibly could be the reason God is not moving in your life. I know there could be many reasons, but do not let this be one. Another verse also comes to mind that states those who show no mercy, there is nothing but judgment (James 2:13). Do not cut your own throat for not being merciful. Do we deceive ourselves with impure motives? Maybe the disciples thought they were helping Jesus when they asked him to call fire from heaven, maybe they thought their motives were pure and their judgment was correct, when in fact it wasn't even close. Please don't be too quick to judge because the measure you measure out will be the measure you will receive.

# LESSON SIX
## *Judgment*

The word *judgment* is defined as the ability to discern the process of forming an opinion based on observation and consideration an option so formed. (Merriam-Webster) However, when God makes a judgment it is not based on an opinion, it is based on facts and it is based on the truth. Jesus told Pilate in John 18:37-38 "Thou says I am a king. To this end was I born, for this cause came I into the world, I should bear witness unto the truth. Everyone that is of the truth heareth my voice. Pilate said unto Him what is truth? In John 14:6 reads, "Jesus sayeth unto Him I am the way, the truth and the life, no man cometh unto the Father but by me." Therefore, Jesus not only bears witness to the truth, He *is* the truth. Therefore, since He is the truth, all his judgments are based on fact, not guesswork or public opinion. Therefore, when God judges us, He is never wrong. Remember that when things go wrong in your life no matter how unfair you think it is, if it does not agree with God, He is not the one making mistakes in judgment, we are. Things are not always as they appear; a young woman I met could not find a job for a year, she lost her apartment, her car and her job, which she lost because she would not sleep with her boss. She told me she quit praying because God was not helping her. I explained to her there could be many reasons she was going through this, but whatever the reason God was not the one in the wrong. I told her you have an enemy! She seemed perplexed, even fearful and asked who her enemy--- was and I told her the devil was. He hates you. She was more perplexed; she asked why does he hate me? I told her it is not personal, he hates all of God's children. He comes to steal, kill and destroy. I then explained to be a Christian is to be like Christ. How can you love your enemy if you have none?

Most people do not understand that they are in a war, a spiritual war, until death. It is not a game; it is a fight to the death. Anyway, I prayed for her and asked one of my friends to pray for her. Two weeks later, she called me asking for a ride. She received a phone call to come for an interview. She filled out the application to be a cook or cashier, but she came out beaming, they offered her a management job. The real kicker, her former boss who tried to sleep with her, also tried it with another girl and lost his job. How that is for judgment? Right before she told me about any of this, I had told her about the scripture which says, "He, who sets a trap, will themselves fall into it." (Psalm 7:15). Her eyes lit up as she told about her former boss losing his job. It reminded me of the story when Haman tried to have Mordecai hung, and ended up, hung himself. Because we serve a great God no one can get over on us when we stay true to God. If they seemingly do, it will only be to elevate us. He is good and His mercy endures forever (Psalm 136).

# CHAPTER SIX
## *God's Way is Higher than Our Ways*

After that relationship, I had a couple more relationships that did not last very long. Then I met the lady I would marry and thought I would spend the rest of my life with, but that is not what happened. She was working at the Winn-Dixie I had just left to move on to another job. We only dated six months and then we were married.

You ever know that you were doing the wrong thing and did it anyway? That is what I did. Many people told me not to marry this person, even the pastor, but I would not listen. Even though I knew they were right. However, I somehow convinced myself it would be alright. You know, kind of like when God told Adam and Eve not to eat of the forbidden fruit. Then Satan came along and said "I know God said not to eat, but it will be alright." Wrong answer. I was trying to know God and she was not really that interested. We were like day and night. She had baggage from living in the home of an alcoholic father and I had my rejection complex. It did not mix too well if you know what I mean. She was a good person; she just did not have the same desires I had. I really do not want to say much about her life, that is her story… but I want to concentrate on my own life.

I will only say we were very different and we spent thirteen miserable years together. I had made up my mind to stick it out no matter what, but she had other plans that did not include me. I believed God used this period of my life to help me grow spiritually and mature in the faith. We had three children during our thirteen years together. We had two sons and a daughter, Aaron, Daniel and Chasity.

# BROKEN PIECES

I will try and explain some of the ways God was helping me to grow during that time. One of the things I remember was God taking the focus off of receiving love from others and giving love regardless of whether you are loved in return. I remember pouring out my heart, telling God how she should love me, but God would not hear it. He told me to love her and that is all I can do. You cannot get someone to love you no matter how much you want to have it happen. This was extremely hard for me to love with nothing in return. It seemed like the more I tried to love her, the worst things got. I am not going to tell you I did not fall short, because it would not be the truth. I can say with all honesty I did the best I knew how, but it just never worked.

During the time that our second child was about to be born, the doctor told us that there was a problem during the pregnancy. He said my son would be born retarded (*an acceptable term back then*) and we should have an abortion. I did not want a retarded child, but I believed abortion was wrong. It shows what you really believe, when you have to make a choice. I thought at one time there was no question what I would do. However, when that doctor said my child was going to be retarded, I struggled with that for a minute, but I held fast to my conviction.

After the physician told us to have an abortion I decided to get a second opinion, the only opinion that matters, the opinion of The Great Physician, Jesus. Whenever my son gave me a little trouble while he was growing up, I would joke with him and say, "You know the doctor said something was wrong with you when you were born," we both get a good laugh. I hear people do a lot of talking about what they would or would not do, but you never really know until it is right in front of you. Some people talk a good game, but when the game is on the line, they run and hide. I know the only way to be faithful is by the grace of God. His word says "without me you can do nothing."(John 15:5) God showed me the truth of that scripture many times during my life.

Early in my marriage I started a new job. The way I got this job

## *God's Ways are Higher than Our Ways*

shows how Gods hand is always in my life. Like I said earlier, I loved sports. We had some friends that we would meet every weekend and play football. One of my other friends started dating this young lady and her brother started playing ball with us. His dad just happened to be the plant manager of the company I would soon work for. I do not believe in coincidences, I believe God specifically places people in your life to fulfill His purpose for your life. I worked at this company for about six years, during this time I was learning a lot about God through studying and reading books about God. I also read a lot of self-help books that were really no help at all. They have some good advice but do not give the power you need to live it. That is what the word of God says about having a form of Godliness but no power; only the word of God and His Spirit can enable us to live right, there is no other way. I can tell you the truth of this by Gods word and by experience.

During the six years I worked there, I started talking to people about God and what I was learning. Many people made fun of me and sometimes I wanted to quit! That was the last thing I wanted after being made fun of all during school. However, I realized that people are going to talk about you whether you are talking about God or not. At least this was a worthwhile thing to be talked about. I worked on the midnight shift. The other shifts called our shift the "God squad." They had a good time laughing at us. However, some of them gave their lives to God and even though I did not know that much about God myself, God still used my feeble efforts. To Him be the Glory!

One time while I was working there, I dropped a very expensive piece of equipment. It cost about fifteen thousand ($15,000) dollars. I did not realize it at the time but when it fell off the cart I was pushing it on, it damaged the seal area and they had to scrap it. My boss asked me what happened and I said "I do not know", but as soon as I said that I remembered I dropped it. I had a choice to tell him I dropped it and probably lose my job (which was one of the best jobs in the area) or I could lie. Without hesitation, I told him I dropped it. I believe God honored me telling the truth. They did not do anything to me at all. I passed the test, which at the time I really did not see it as such. However, as I look back at my life there were many such times. God is waiting for your response but not for His sake, but for yours. He already knew what I was going to do. He wanted to let me know.

I worked there until about 1986. Then I was laid off. I had two children and one on the way. However, three years before this I had purchased a house, which was another way God was teaching me about faith. Before we purchased the house, God gave me the faith to believe we were going to buy a house. Then, all the circumstances said it was not going to happen. Somehow I just knew that house was going to be ours. Yes, we got the house. We lived in that house about three years. One day I was out in the yard minding my business. God showed up, out of nowhere, when I least expected. This may sound strange to some, as it was to me at the time. It was like someone dropped a veil over my head. I could physically feel this….don't ask, I can't explain it! All I know is that with this feeling came a distinct knowing that I would soon be moving…out of state.

The next thing I know, I am moving to Georgia. I had been laid off for a year. We always got by. God only knows how. I moved to Georgia with my father-in-law. We were going to move our families to Georgia once we got jobs. We originally intended to go to Dalton, GA but the day before we left he received a phone call out of the blue from one of his relatives. It just so happened, that he said he could get us a job where he worked, so we moved to Conyers, GA instead. I got the job he mentioned, but only worked there for one week. The place I moved to is where I actually met someone who told me about the place where he worked, that was hiring. A few days before I met him, I was riding down one of the streets in town and noticed this huge company and made the comment to myself that I wanted to work at a place like that.

I did not even know what they did, but it turned out that this was the exact place the guy I met told me about. God has a good sense of humor…out of all the places I could have named or pointed out in that town, I just happened to point out the one I would soon be

## God's Ways are Higher than Our Ways

working for…fat chance! I worked there for the next eight years! There was also a monastery in the town where I lived. I spent a lot of time there and met many people who influenced my spiritual growth tremendously. I was really hungry for the knowledge of God. I met a man who told me something I never forgot. A very simple statement, that I found over the years to have a lot of truth to it. He said, "You'll have many acquaintances during life but very few real friends." I always tell people this now, that if you ever find a real true friend make sure you treasure them. There are not that many genuine ones (friends) left. I have been fortunate to have a few, but I have also been a good friend to people.

The word of God says if you want friends show yourself friendly. It will come back to you eventually. However, I have also had my share of people I have helped that stabbed me in the back…more than my share actually. I can loan you some of them if you would like. I did not think so. During the eight years I worked for this company, my marriage was getting worst by the day. However, I kept seeking God's face and witnessed to everyone I worked with. There were about four or five hundred people working there. During the eight years, at one time or another, I told every one of them about the God I served, even though I had not experienced many of the things I would soon experience. I took it one step at a time. God was giving me some on-the-job training. In addition, during this time I went through a very severe trial, one that I never, ever want to repeat. I knew in my heart that I was putting my children before God. I knew because I had a lot of anxiety about losing my children. I knew even though I was doing everything I knew to save my marriage, it was still falling apart. Then one day I was talking to God and told him, "I know I have my children before you, but I desire to have you first in my life." This would be one of those times you wished you had never opened your mouth. God answered this sooner than I thought He would, but the process I went through to get there was a nightmare for me. Right after I said that to God, someone called the Family and Children Services and told them a bunch of lies, saying we were abusing our children.

# BROKEN PIECES

I know the way we got along was harmful to my children, and it made them nervous to see their parents not getting along, but as far as us hurting them or abusing them, was an outright lie. I had heard all these stories of children being taken by Family and Children Services. Even though I knew, we were not abusing our children. I knew if I told them how we, my wife and I got along, they might take my children and put them in someone's home with God only knows what kind of people. I had a lot of fear going on inside of me not because I was hurting my children, but because of all the stories I had heard. This went on for months with these people coming around asking all kinds of questions. Even though I knew telling them the truth about me and my wife's relationship could cost me my children, I told the truth. This is what I believe with all my heart is what God allowed to test me to see if I would put Him first by telling the truth and facing a real possibility of losing my children. It probably was not true but in my mind, it was.

This was one of the worst things I ever went through in my entire life. This situation kept replaying over and over in my mind. Then one day at church, the leader of our prayer group suggested we write down whatever it was we needed to let go of and give to God. Then he told us to fold it up and put in a helium balloon, and let it go, symbolically giving our burdens, cares and troubles over to God. I wrote the names of my three children and turned it over into His hands. If you don't know, God has very big hands! He can hold whatever weight that is weighing you down. The next day Family and Children Services came by the house and they informed me they would no longer be coming to my home. We serve an amazing God. I thanked God it was over and I remembered as I meditated on those things that had just taken place in my life, I could not help but think about Abraham placing Isaac on the altar. Although God was not asking me to take the life of my children, the thought of losing them was like a thousand deaths to me. From that experience I learned that whatever we as people have in our lives, especially the things or people we love the most will have to be placed on the altar; there are no exceptions. God must have first place in your heart. I have learned that everything God gives us, we must have with open hands. The more we try to

## God's Ways are Higher than Our Ways

hold on, the more it eludes us. God's purpose was not to make me afraid but to set me free from what was in control of my heart. He must control our heart nothing else. God wants us to enjoy the things he places in our life, not be imprisoned by them. Do you have anxiety about losing things? If you do you are enslaved by it. Give it to God, you will never enjoy it or have peace as long as it controls you. Remember God loves you more than you love yourself. Anything can control you, money, power, pleasure, people, sports, etc. I know it is scary but let it go. Put your trust in the one who knows all from beginning to the end. God said He is the Alpha and Omega, let Him be yours. His hands are better than Allstate, and his insurance is free!

# LESSON SEVEN
## The Peace of God

Peace is defined as freedom from hostility, and being in complete serenity. (Merriam-Webster) That is the peace of the world, not the peace of God. The way I define peace, is that stillness in the center of your being (your heart) caused by order that is the result of having Jesus on the throne of your heart. Where there is order, there is peace. "Peace, I leave with you, my peace I give unto you, not as the world giveth, give I unto you. Let not your heart be troubled, neither let it be afraid. (John 14:27)

Are you searching for peace? There is only one place you will find it. We have peace with God by being reconciled to Jesus Christ. Not even Donald Trump with all his money can buy one ounce of true peace. There is no one else no matter how much fame, power or charisma they posses can give you any peace… and if they say they can offer you this peace and security that only comes from a relationship with Jesus Christ, run from them! There is only one way to receive peace and that is the gift of God. In addition, there is only one way to lose it, and that is to freely give it away. The devil cannot take it, your mama, your daddy, your wife, the government, etc., no one can take it from you, and you can only receive it or give it away.

Is Jesus on the throne of your heart, or have you evicted Him by your own will, or your evil desires? Jesus wants all or none, either He's Lord or you are. If it's you that's a very poor choice, and you will never be able to receive His peace. If it is Jesus you will always have this peace you're longing for, and no one can break in and steal it from you. Aren't you tired of trying to protect and keep yourself from harm? *You should be*, because it is an impossible task.

I said in the beginning peace comes from order, do you have your life in order? This is the order: God first in every area of your life. Who's Lord in your life? Is it your boss, your paycheck, your friends, your reputation? God must be first; not your favorite sporting event. Some may call you a religious fanatic not realizing how they themselves are fanatical about everything but God. *(Sorry Tiger or Lebron)* only God can give you true peace. Neither can their paychecks give them peace! That's why most people with a lot of money, but no God, are miserable and have no peace. Let Jesus handle your money and every aspect of your life. I am not saying you can't have money and peace, but those who leave God out of their lives will, without a doubt, have no peace.

It only takes one thing to rob you of peace. Remember the story of the rich young ruler who said, "Master what must I do to have eternal life?", and Jesus told him to keep all the commandments", he thought, *well I have*, but then Jesus said, "Oh by the way there is one more thing, go take all that money that took you your whole life to make and give it to the poor, and then come follow me." Quite a big order; there is one thing I'm certain of, until he dealt with that, he never could receive the peace Jesus offered. There is a price no matter which side you choose. He could lose his money or lose eternity. What is your choice? Jesus said you cannot serve two masters, you have to choose. The wisest choice is Jesus, but so many are unable to make that choice. What I really mean is not *unable*, but unwilling. Therefore, I plead with you to make the wise choice, because nothing will ever be able to satisfy that emptiness inside of you that only God can fill. In most cases, I

## *God's Ways are Higher than Our Ways*

believe God will not only give you back what you gave up, but more. Actually, in all cases, but it may not be the thing you gave up. If He doesn't give back what you gave up, you'll never miss it, because He will give you something better.

It is not that God wants to take something from you, but only those things that steal your affections from Him. Abraham not only got his son back, but also the peace of knowing nothing was before his God. You can never enjoy something that holds you prisoner. So, open the gates and let the King of Glory come in. There is also another side of peace, some people want peace at any price, even the price of their soul. Look at Matthew 10:34-36. "Think not that I am come to send peace on earth. I came not to send peace, but a sword for I have come to set a man at variance against his father, and daughter against her mother, and the daughter-in-law against her mother-in-law, and a man's foes shall be them of his own household." Therefore, which is it Jesus wants, peace or war? He wants peace with man and war with anything that steals our affections from God.

Hebrews 12:14 says, "Strive to live in peace with everybody and pursue that consecration and holiness without which no one will ever see the Lord." It says strive to, but we all know there are many people who just don't want peace, they want their way… that will always destroy your peace having it your way, not His. I can hear Jesus knocking at the door of your heart pleading with you to allow Him to remove any and everything that stands between you and God. Open it; you won't be sorry, you will be glad you did. You also have what you can't have any other way, peace. May His peace remain with you all the days of your life. Amen.

One more thing before I move on, what I just wrote is simple to understand, but the process we go through to get from A to Z, can be hell on earth. If it were easy, everyone would be doing it. To let go of things we love is painful, but there is no other way to the other side. Sorry, but I just wanted to make it clear, it's not easy, but worth it. God bless and take courage.

# CHAPTER SEVEN
*Enemies Now Friends*

After that trial was over, I began sharing my faith more than I had previously shared Christ. There was a man I worked with whom I tried to share the gospel with on a few occasions and had little or no success as far as I could see. He wasn't "feeling' it" as they say and he seemed to despise it. My job was delivering parts to assembly line; his was to assemble the product. One day I was delivering some parts to the area he worked in. He dropped a part he was working with and barked at me to pick it up. Now I was the one who wasn't feeling it. If you knew me, you know I don't let people walk all over me…it didn't matter how big and ugly they were. The way he talked to me was very rude. So when he told me to pick it up, I was thinking *"pick it up yourself,"* but I felt God wanted me to humble myself and pick it up, which I did. This same guy had a friend who really liked talking to me, he told me he felt at peace when he was around me. He also informed me that the person that was being rude to me was going through a bad relationship. I wonder why? Anyway, I gave him some tracks (encouraging stories) to give to his friend because I knew he would not accept them from me. When asked where he got those tracks from, the friend told the person I had given them to him. He then told me that after he found out I was the one who gave them to him, after having been so nasty to me; he started crying and gave his heart to God. He became one of my friends. The word of God says, when you love your enemies he will make even your enemies to be at peace with you.

On another occasion the plant manager came up to me and informed me to take down a picture of Jesus I had in my work area. He told me it was not work-related so I had to take it down.

# BROKEN PIECES

What I told him, I am sure he was not expecting. I told him that the pictures of naked women all over the plant were not work-related either. However, I told him I would take it down. An hour later the company posted a letter informing everyone to take down all the nude pictures in the plant. God made his own words come back to bite him. I'm sure he did not all of a sudden fall in love with Jesus. He was probably afraid I would sue him, which had never crossed my mind.

It is just one of those times you just have to look up to heaven and smile. All the people that had to take down their pictures were not smiling; somehow they all seem to know who was responsible, even though I said nothing to them. I would much rather people be angry with me than have God angry with me. The word of God says the fear of man is a snare. Do not be caught in their trap, you will always come out on top when you fear God and not man.

One time there was a young woman that always wore this skirt that said "Party Naked". I told her that kind of thing grieved God and was not pleasing to him. She was not a Christian, so of course she hated me after I told her that. Sometime after she suffered a miscarriage and she was extremely depressed. I gave her a booklet with information about what she was going through. After that she became my friend. Later she even married a Christian and became a believer herself. It is amazing what a little kindness can do. People have to see that you really care about them personally and you are there for them when they are hurting. It also has a lot more punch to it when you are helping someone you know that does not like you. They cannot figure it out but they know it is something different from what they have experienced. It's Gods all consuming love. It changes people, we do not have to figure it out, just accept it and then go and do likewise. You will never regret loving people even though they may never accept it. It may not always change them, but it will always change you.

On another occasion there was a man I worked with that did everything in his power to make me miserable. He was very good at his job; he had a master's degree in the art of antagonizing people. He talked behind my back and in my face; it did not matter to him. He called me names, anything to get under my skin, but the more he tried to irritate me, the more I showed him kindness. He told someone else he could not stand it when I was kind to him. Even though he was being a snake to me, I asked him to go hunting with me. That broke him…because he could not figure out why I would ask him to hunt with him after he had been so nasty. Maybe he thought I was waiting for a good opportunity to put an end to him in the woods, so he declined the offer…. but he eventually gave up trying to be my enemy and became my friend. Love covers a multitude of sins that includes our own, which Jesus covered on the cross. You can take a minute to thank Him now if you would like. Back to the rest of the story as they say.

# LESSON EIGHT
## *The Call*

I believe God calls out to all people, the difference is, many are so busy, or tangled in sin they either do not hear it or do not recognize God is speaking to them. The word of God says many are called, but few are chosen. The reason few are chosen is not because of God, but because we do not respond to it. I believe there is a general calling and a specific calling. The general calling is the way God calls everyone to salvation, and the specific call, is what God calls us to do individually. The word of God says God is not willing that any should perish, but come to everlasting life. Sad, but true, many reject that call therefore, never getting to the second calling.

Paul received his conversion call and specific call simultaneously. The Lord said unto him, "Go thy way for he is a chosen vessel unto me, to bear my name before the Gentiles, and kings and the children of Israel. For I will show him how great things he must suffer for my name's sake" (Act 9:15). Are we willing to suffer for Christ sake to fulfill our calling? This is where many people shrink back, and run from God. Only problem with that is they run into far worst problems trying to run from God, ---*I have been there.* We are a generation of Jonas'. Then we blame God when life swallows us like a whale. Then we stink and are full of fish guts among other things. Then God in his mercy has to do something supernatural to get us back on track. We could have avoided all the pain and heartache if we would just learn from others. Not only do we hurt ourselves, our life affects many other lives as well. We refuse to listen.

Look in the book of Esther 4:14,which says "for if thou altogether holdest thy peace at this time, then shall there enlargement and deliverance arise to the Jews from another place, but thou and thy fathers house shall be destroyed, and who knoweth whether thou art come to the kingdom for such a time as this?" What Mordecai was saying, in a nutshell, is this, do what God has called you to do or he will use someone else, but you will pay a heavy price for your rejection of God's call for you to do this. This is very serious business; God calls us specifically for a reason. God does not like to waste His time and investment He put in us. I sense the fear of God just talking about this. I talk more about this fear of God later. God paid a heavy price for us. He did not get us from a yard sale for a couple of dollars. He paid for us with the precious blood of Christ. If you are hearing His call, answer the door. He stands at the door and knocks; do not act like it is a salesman at the door…seeing Him coming, turning out all the lights and being as quiet as a mouse. This is the King of Glory, let Him come in. This is my prayer, let Him in, you will not be sorry. I can tell you from personal experience of the pain that was unnecessary, had I listened, but I will get to that later.

# LESSON NINE
## *Ministry*

This is the office and duties of a minister, a department of government or the building in which it is housed, the care of others. The first thing I would like to point out is that everyone God calls, is called to some type of ministry. There is one thing for sure, we will never find out what that ministry is if we never look or ask God what it is He has called us to do. The simplest way to start out is to obey the word of God. God will not give us step two, if we never take, step one. Walk in the light as He is in the light. The more we are obedient to God's word, the more clearly it will be known what is it that God has called us to do. If we half-heartedly obey God, we will never understand or fulfill God's call for ministry in our life. God wants all, not a few crumbs.

Everyone is called to minister the word of God in some capacity. I've heard people say I do not tell people about God, I just show it by my life. That's like buying something and the instructions only have pictures, but do not tell you how they work together. I believe the real reason is fear. Some people fear they will be rejected or they do not know what to say. Neither of these will stand. First of all what they are really rejecting is God, not you. You are only the instrument God is using to bring His truth to light. The other excuse is you do not know what say; well you have all the knowledge on the inside of you. Jesus said He would give you what to say. In addition, we should study to show ourselves approved rightly dividing the word of truth (2 Timothy 2:15). There are people all around us dying and possibly on their way to hell that need a word from God. It seems to me as though your ministry will always have something to do with things you have gone through, that way you are better able to sympathize (and empathize) with them and understand their struggles. A word of caution, some people who, say for example, had a drinking problem want to help those with similar struggles, that's great, but how you go about it makes all the difference in the world. Zig Ziegler, a Christian motivational speaker, said "Every once in a while you find a good biscuit in the garbage can, but that's not where you go looking for one." So do not fool yourself and say you are going to help the alcoholic by hanging out at the bar. God will make sure you have plenty of opportunities without going to places that will lead you right back into bondage. Remember, this will be worse than the first time you were in bondage. Use wisdom when you minister. Satan is always looking for a way to destroy you, your testimony or both. Wherever you minister, do it with the right attitude or it won't benefit you or the person you're ministering to. People see right through falsehood. One kind word is worth more than all the money, fame, or whatever you could achieve, when it is done in love. Love should be your main, if not only motive. People are really searching for someone who really cares.

I know there have been many times people have done something for me or helped me with impure motives out of guilt. Those times are not even worth getting help when you know in your heart they really do not care. It also makes it hard to accept a gift though you really need it, when it wasn't done in love. So if your motive isn't love do not waste your time giving it. I am not talking about your feelings because sometimes you really want to help someone but you don't feel like it. Say for example your wife wakes you up in the middle of the night sick and asks you to go out to Wal-Mart and get her some medicine. You might want to go, but you can't convince your body you want to, but you do it anyway. Jesus didn't exactly jump for joy the night before being nailed to the cross for us, but He did it. People do not always say what they feel, but their lives are really touched by the sacrifices you make for them. Especially when they know they do not deserve it… by the way, none of us deserves it, but God loves us anyway. Get out your oil and start oiling those rusty parts you haven't used in years. Yes, years for some, many years, so get out and help someone. You will be glad you did. Get those seeds out and start sowing. God promises a great harvest.

# CHAPTER EIGHT
*Tempted & Tried*

As time passed I began to get really weary and felt like giving up. It was not that I did not believe, I just got burned out. You ever been there, perhaps you are there now. Don't quit, just rest. I told God, "I give up... I can't take it anymore." Then a book company I had ordered some books from before sent me a book I didn't order. They said I had sent them too much money. The book was about six inches thick and from cover to cover was all about the reality of hell and revelations of people that were in hell. I couldn't sleep for about a week after I read it.

If people ever put any deep thought into eternity they would make some changes, but Satan is very good at getting our focus off of eternity and making us think only of here and now. After I read the book, things didn't all of a sudden become easier; Satan came in like a flood to drown me. This was about a year before my wife divorced me. There was a woman next door who started showing me a lot of attention and made it clear, that if I was willing she was able. At this time in my life I had been through 12 years of a horrible marriage, and was getting no attention from my wife....at least not the kind a man wants from his wife anyway. Satan comes at your weakest points and tries to do you a favor; of course, he conveniently forgets to tell you he is trying to destroy your life and your place in eternity, which he has already lost. He wants some company, misery loves company. I was in my mid-thirties and this woman was 24, beautiful and married. The fact that she was married didn't seem to be a problem for her either. She used every technique in her arsenal to bring me into her fold and put an end to this "God stuff." She even went as far as saying, "If God is merciful, won't he forgive you?" I said "Yes, He will forgive me, after He beats me like a red headed stepchild."

# BROKEN PIECES

I didn't know a whole lot, but I knew God would correct us severely because we knew better. I knew better but at the same time I was hurting and starving for comfort and affection. Because of the state of mind I was in I let it go on much longer than I should have. You keep playing with fire you will surely get burned. Satan had me by one hand and God had me by the other; one promising comfort now and the other one later. My heart convicted me so much I couldn't stand it. I finally told her "you're beautiful and I like talking to you, but you're not worth going to hell for…don't ever come to my house again." I never saw her again.

It wasn't easy to walk away, even though I knew it was wrong. I told God, "Ok, I've done the right thing. I didn't sleep with her, but I need some help here, I'm really hurting inside." About six months went by, and things only seemed to get worse. I cried out to God, "Where are you?", but there was nothing but silence… and this is where most people call it quits.

## LESSON TEN
### *Hatred of Sin*

This is something that is not talked about very much these days, but is something we must grow in as we come closer to God. How many people you know really hate their sin or weaknesses? Not many. If they did, they would not be enjoying watching it on TV every night. They wouldn't be laughing or joking about it. Just as much as God loves righteousness, He hates sin. In Psalm 97:10 the word says, "O you, who love the Lord, hate evil." He preserves the lives of His saints; He delivers them out of the hand of the wicked one. You cannot love the Lord and evil at the same time. Sometimes we fool ourselves, we say we love God, but our lives talk with a different tongue. I've seen many people who claim to love God and hate sin, but still have a secret affair with their sin, sometimes to our shame, openly. I worked with a man who professed to being a servant of God, and he was also talking to people, sharing his faith. One day I noticed him looking on with a co-worker at some pictures of naked women that the co-worker had taken in Florida on vacation. I confronted him about it, and he became defensive and said there was nothing wrong with that... but to his defense I will say, he later came back and admitted it was wrong and repented. You say how can you hate sin? What does it look like? Well what does it look like when you hate people, or spinach or whatever else it is you hate? Well you have absolutely nothing to do with it, you don't think about it except when you want to vent your hatred towards it. When you see someone you hate you will walk an extra block or mile to avoid them. When it comes to sin we get as close to it as possible so we can smell it, breathe it, and embrace it without it taking us captive. When we are that close we're already in the cell and all Satan has to do is close the door and lock it.

When we are so captivated by sin, we will never notice it until it's too late. The reason I know this is because I have had the door slammed on me more than I would like to admit. We usually don't learn until sin has cost us something. It cost me plenty, but that's when you begin to hate your sin, when you realize how much it cost you or someone you love. Your sin and mine, cost Jesus to be crucified on the cross. That's a high price to pay, but thank God, He paid it, and paid it in full. If Jesus had not paid the price, we would all be without hope. Without hope is not a good place to be, trust me friend you don't want to be there. I believe that is one of the worst things we can suffer, is to know all the times God called out to us and we refused, because we loved our sin more. The regret is unbearable, just knowing the things we should have turned away from and didn't...and how it cost us or the people we love something as well. So please stay as far from sin as you possibly can and pray I do the same. It is our nature to love sin and as horrible as it sounds, that is the truth. We must cry out for the grace of God to cause us to hate sin and love righteousness.

There is one other thing I would like to share about the hatred of sin. It is found in Luke 14:26: "If any man come to me, and hate not his father and mother, and wife, and children, and brother, and sisters, and his own life also, he cannot be my disciple." Which is it? One minute God is telling us to love and the next he is telling us to hate… we have to do both. We must love them as God loves them, but hate, as far as coming in between you and God, or God's will for your life is concerned. Are these people idols in our life, do we compromise our faith for our family? Do you allow your children to go places, hangout with the wrong people to keep the peace? If we do, the price will be far more than you will want to pay. What we are doing is actually not for them, it's against them, and will eventually destroy their lives, or relationships. I have had to do many things that my children or family were not very pleased with. I will tell you what I had to tell them. "When I die, it's not going to be me and you standing before God, but me and God alone. I want His approval more than yours." The word of God says, "Don't fear man who can kill the body, but fear God who can throw both body and soul into hell." (Matthew 10:28) I think I will go with God, how about you? It is your choice, but you will have to live with it forever. Make the right choice; choose life you will be glad you did. May God's peace be with you. Amen!

# LESSON ELEVEN
*Entertainment or Entertain*

Entertainment means to amuse, to offer hospitality, to consider as an ideal or proposal. (Merriam-Webster)Now you say what does this have to do with God? That is a good question. Are the things we as the people of God do to entertain ourselves, healthy for us spiritually? We watch things that are anti-God nonstop on TV; see movies that should make us cringe, and listen to music that is demeaning. All the things God says He hates, we're laughing and making a joke about it. You continually watch TV shows about people cheating, and being cheated on, and think nothing of it. What if it was your wife that was cheating? I do not think that would be very entertaining. I met a man at work who was laughing about cheating on his wife, and had the nerve to say if he caught her cheating he would do this or that to her. I told him what makes it any different for him. I also told him he was sick. I normally watch my words but sometimes you have to lay it out there in bold print, to make people see themselves. He thought cheating was a big joke and probably watched it on TV a million times. God does not think its funny one bit. How many marriages, relationships are destroyed by imitating what we call entertainment? I'm not saying we can't do anything to entertain ourselves, but it should be done with God in the picture. Would you take Jesus with you to the movies you watch? If you can't, you shouldn't go. The word of God says to think on things that are pure, lovely and of good report.

Probably 95 percent of what most people call entertainment, God calls wicked or evil. Make sure whatever your entertaining yourself with, you can find it in your Bible *or at least* not find it with God saying how evil it is. If we, as the people of God, had a good relationship with God not only would we not do some or most of the things we do to entertain ourselves, we would not want to. If we have to constantly entertain ourselves, it shows we are empty inside looking for something to fill that void inside of us. Only God can fill any void inside of us. So many people are always searching for something or someone to fill that emptiness inside of us when the only thing that can, is on the inside of us already.

People are dying on the inside when the one and only one who died for them has died for a relationship with them, one that can fill all that emptiness. I've searched other places to find contentment but came up empty, and so will you. The only place you'll find real peace and contentment is in the blood stained hands of the one who died for you. Let me save you the pain and loss you'll experience if you go looking somewhere else. People are making millions of dollars to destroy your life. Keep your money and invest it into the kingdom of God. You will be happy, and also the people around you, not to mention the joy you'll bring to your Savior. There is so much more to a relationship with God than people realize. Some people do not know because they have never been taught there is more. Some people think it is not exciting enough. Some people point blank, just do not care about anyone but themselves.

# BROKEN PIECES

Many people do not realize this until it is too late or their lives are shattered. If they live at all, they live with regret. Invest your life into other people. It is the only real value meal. I've talked to so many people looking for something to fulfill them, when the only real investment is other people's lives. So many people are touched by the smallest acts of kindness when it is done in love. People can see real love. People really want to be loved, not entertained. So, let's quit wasting our time with some or most of the empty things, we call entertainment.

## LESSON TWELVE
### *Superstition*

Superstition is defined as an irrational belief, any practice inspired by such a belief. (Merriam-Webster) The reason I am including this in the list of topics, is because I find that many people including Christians have some of this operating in their life… it is not of God. Many people think it is harmless, but they unwillingly open their lives to many dangers. I was riding in my car one day, and a black cat ran in front of my car, the person riding with me, told me to stop and turn around, and they meant it. They said its bad luck; I said "yeah, bad luck for the cat if he is not fast enough." All the men said "Make my day!", and the women said "You are so mean!" I was just joking; do not turn me into the humane society.

There are many other myths, such as Horoscope, Palm Reading, Mediums (talking to the dead), finding a penny upside down, bad luck walking under a ladder, etc. If I find a $100 dollar bill upside down, it might be bad luck for the one who lost it, but good luck for me. Seriously, I do not believe anything happens by luck, but as a result of the choices, we make, or other people make. Whatever a man sows so shall he reap. If things happened, by luck, God would be unjust and it is not going to happen. So be careful what you believe and make sure it is based on truth, which is the word of God. Do not wait for your hand to itch thinking you will receive money. Scratch your knees on the floor and pray that our great God will supply all of your needs!

# CHAPTER NINE
*Filled*

I decided to visit this ministry in Alabama, where one of the pastors listened to me pour my heart out to him. He listened and then said he would like to pray for me. I never turned down prayer. I needed some help desperately. He anointed me with oil and prayed over me. At the time that he was praying for me, I felt nothing. The next day when I went to work and it was like someone swapped bodies with me. Instead of feeling depressed and miserable, I was full of joy and peace. This was new for me and I liked it, but I was waiting for it to end. A month went by and I still had this joy, peace and love for people that I never knew existed. I didn't know it at the time, but God had filled me with His Holy Spirit.

One day I was walking around at work and the thought came to me to pray for the gift of tongues. The church I attended never talked about those things. Although, some did believe in speaking in tongues and practiced it. I had never heard anyone speak in tongues and I knew very little about it. I had a co-worker who would tell me about praying in the Spirit. I had no idea what he was talking about. I later found out he was talking about this speaking-in-tongues thing. I asked him to pray with me for this gift, not knowing what to expect. He started out praying in English and then went off into God only knows what language. When he was through praying somehow I just knew in my spirit or in your gut as they say that I had received it even though I had not prayed in another language. I went home that night and I actually could speak in another language. For about 3 weeks I had a war going on inside of me. Part of me believing it was real and part of me thinking I was making it up. There were times when I could pray in tongues and times when I could not. When my co-worker prayed he was unhindered. I told him about the struggle I was having. He told me sometimes we are just not yielding to the Holy Spirit. I asked if he could pray for me again. We were at work on break, when he told me to raise my hands. I felt a bit ridiculous, but I did it.

What would follow was totally unexpected. Have you ever seen the cartoons when someone gets hit over the head and sees stars spinning over their head? Well as my co-worker was praying I could visibly see about six inches in front of me, syllables of letters spinning like that in front of me. When I went home that night I was indeed able to pray in the spirit and speak in tongues. I was no more in doubt about the realty of speaking in tongues. It became a normal part of my prayer life from that day forward. This was one of many supernatural experiences I have had. Not everyone is excited about gifts of the Spirit; some even think you have lost your mind. I understand because before I experienced it for myself, I thought some of the same things. I realized there is a whole spirit world around us that most people have no idea even exists. You will never find it until you seek it with your whole heart. The word of God says he gives his Spirit to those who obey him (Act 5:32).

Soon after this, I met a young man who was addicted to drugs and many other bad habits. He was real kind, but was really struggling with many addictions. I shared my new experience with him. I could tell he wanted a change in his life. I asked him if he wanted to come to church with me. I felt in my heart it was urgent for him to give his life to God. He declined my offer to come to church because he said he was waiting on a phone call about a job. I told him to put God first and come to church, but his faith was too weak to believe that God would take care of him. I could sense the Spirit of God convicting him to come with me to church and as I was about to turn and leave he reached out and hugged me as if he was afraid this would be his last chance to give his life over to God. For some it may be the last time salvation is offered to them. We never know when our last chance will come, so please don't put off accepting Christ. A short time passed and I found out he had been arrested for drugs. I saw him about a year later, he told me he had given his life to God; was filled with the joy of Christ and had his life back on track. I thank God it wasn't too late for him. To God be the Glory!

# LESSON THIRTEEN
## *The Joy of the Lord*

The dictionary defines joy as intense happiness or pleasure; the cause of such pleasure. This intense happiness or pleasure comes not as a result of what we have or don't have, but who we have or don't have. In Galatians 5:22 it says, "But the fruit of the Spirit is love, joy, peace, long-suffering, gentleness, goodness, faith, meekness, and temperance; against such things, there is no law." Do you have the fruit of the Spirit?

When Jesus is on the inside, ruling you, you will experience unspeakable joy, and be full of the glory of God. If you don't, you will be full of something else which I won't mention. If you've lost your joy, seek God and ask Him what you have allowed to enter your life that has stolen your joy. You know that Satan comes to steal, kill, and destroy. The word says he comes, but you are the one who gives him the key, that's right, you freely give him your joy. What are some of the keys we give him? One key we give him is sin. Your joy will leave you faster than Satan was thrown out of heaven if you start getting into sin. Remember, joy is one of the fruits of the Spirit. Whenever we sin we grieve the Spirit of God; grieving and joy cannot abide in you at the same time. There is pleasure in sin, but only for a season, then it turns to bitterness. There are certain foods which are very sweet when you first bite into it, but after it settles in your stomach it turns sour or bitter. Sin has a similar reaction.

Whenever we sin, we will always hit bottom, it's not *if* we will hit bottom, but when. When you hit there is going to be a big mess. This is when we either beg God to help us, or blame Him for our mess that we freely chose to bring upon ourselves. Remember we gave Satan the key, and he is going to use it as long as it's in his possession. We have to repent and take our key back.

The second key we give the enemy of our souls that can rob us of our joy, is the key of doubt. Whenever we begin to doubt God's word concerning our lives, our joy goes right out the window. Whenever we don't believe God, our hearts are filled with anxiety… joy and anxiety *doesn't* mix well. It's one or the other, make your choice. When you choose to believe God, you'll have joy, when you don't, misery takes over. Which one do you want? It's your choice.

The third key is thankfulness, are you using this key, or are you whining and complaining? Try to stop complaining and whining, and start being thankful! It may not change your situation, but it will change you, and more than likely your situation down the road. Think about it, what good does complaining do, except make you and everyone around you miserable? Whenever you are miserable, you are more than likely to compromise your values and integrity. Then your problems really seem to manifest. I remember once, my son was a small child when this happened. He got into a big hole at a nearby park, and he couldn't get out. I used his unfortunate accident as an opportunity to teach him about life. I told him it's real easy to get in a hole, but not as easy to get out of one. He's still learning that one. I believe we have all gotten ourselves in some hole where we find ourselves with great regrets. However, if you get yourself into a hole, please cry out to God. Weeping may last for a night, but joy comes in the morning. (Psalm 30:5)Stand guard over your heart, and let His joy be your strength, you will be glad you did.

# LESSON FOURTEEN
## Unanswered Prayer

This is a subject that could be talked about for as long as we live. The aspect I would like to focus on is that of unanswered prayer. The word of God says we should pray according to His will, but not only His goodwill, but His specific will for our life. Let us say for example, you are praying to be a great baseball player and you pray God "help me catch the ball; help me hit the ball," and all the different aspects of the game you would like to be proficient in. Time passes, and you get worse and worse at the game. Bottom line, you stink at baseball. There is nothing wrong or sinful in and of itself in playing ball. When we do not get our prayer answered, we get angry at God, we quit praying and some even, *God forbid* deny God is real. We tread on dangerous ground when we allow our understanding to become a stumbling block when our prayers are not answered the way we think they should be.

Remember someone named Job got himself in a little hot water when he questioned God's way of doing things. This is my version of what God said to Job, "Ok Mr. Smarty Pants, since you know so much, where were you when I laid the foundations of the earth, declare if you have understanding." (Job 38:4). Have you ever stopped to think that God never called him to be a baseball player, not that there is anything wrong with it. God called him to be an evangelist. Therefore why would God, an all knowing God at that, help him to be a great ball player if that was not God's will for his life. Don't get me wrong, if God wanted him to be a great baseball player it would come to pass. However when we focus on wanting our way, we become blinded to the will of God. We are so focused on our way we lose His way. Remember we are followers of Christ not leaders of Christ. It's not our will, but His that matters. We must die to our will in favor of God's will.

A loving Father is going to give you the right equipment for the job he has called you to do. What if your dad told you he was going to teach you how to play baseball, then threw you a football to learn with. Something is wrong with this picture. Remember God is answering with the full picture in view. This is one of the many reasons God does not answer the way we think He should and many are frustrated their entire life. This had me frustrated and blaming God for quite some time. So once again, we must not only pray for God's will, but God's will for our life specifically. Even when we know His specific will for our life we do not know all of the details ourselves. God knows how much of this and how much of that each of us needs. We think we know but we do not. We are His sheep and sheep are dumb… *and* they stink too.

Let us say you were praying for healing to be able to walk. I believe it is God's perfect will for you to walk, but God knows that if you do walk, you will walk away from Him, not because you have to, (but remember He knows the beginning from the end), but because you choose to. Would you heal your child if you knew he would walk out on the street and get run over? God knows the choices we will make before we make them. So being a loving Father He would never give us something (though it may be good in and of itself) that would ultimately destroy us or be in opposition to His will for our life. He knows if we will use His gifts correctly, with this fore knowledge He possesses. He answers accordingly. In a nutshell, God not only knows what you can do but what you will do. Therefore, instead of being mad at God for not getting what you pray for, you should be thanking Him. He knows what is best for your life.

I believe God takes every aspect of our life, our choices, weaknesses, character, and answers accordingly. He knows not only about all the things in our life, but how we will manifest those things throughout our life. He works these things in our life to shape and mold us. For example, let us say God sees pride in your life that you do not see, that is why you probably think you know more than God in the first place. He knows just what to allow in your life to drive pride out, how little and how much. So, trust God with your life. Trust in the Lord with all your heart and lean not onto your own understanding, acknowledge Him in all, yes all your ways and He will direct your path. He is all good, praise His wonderful name!

# CHAPTER TEN
## *Led by the Spirit*

Like I said before, not everyone gets excited about your new view of life. My wife became more against me than ever. One day we got in an argument, the next thing I know she had packed up and taken my three kids and moved out of state to live with her sister in Tennessee. I prayed for my marriage but she never returned, then she divorced me.

By this time, I had been through many trials and I was learning to trust God's judgments over my own. A few months before my wife left I had made a cross out of some aluminum framing of a window screen and nailed it to a tree in my backyard. I came outside after a thunderstorm and lightning had struck the tree and cut it in half. I said to myself, "that's not a very good sign." I had read a story about how when sin becomes too great in your life, it's like the root of a tree. It goes deep into our lives and if you try and pull it out it will kill the tree. So, instead cut it down and plant another tree beside it and overshadow the other tree.

The word of God says that which is born of the flesh is flesh and that which is born of the spirit is spirit (John 3:6). So in like manner we have two different root systems within each of us, our (natural man) the root born of the flesh and our (spirit man) the root born of the Spirit. After the lightning hit the tree I had nailed the cross in, I went across the street and dug up an oak tree out in the woods behind my neighbor's home. After I planted the tree, which I had planted to reflect my life, it looked like it wasn't going to make it. The leaves started getting full of mold and shriveling up. Then on top of that, the wind had blown this huge tree behind the tree I planted, and it was leaning over the tree I planted. If this tree behind the tree I planted were to fall, it would fall right on top of the tree I planted. Because I had planted the tree as a symbolic representation of my life, and it looked like it was dying, and about to be smashed by another huge tree, this fear came over me. I felt, just like the tree I planted wasn't going to make it, neither was I. As this fear hovered over me like the giant David killed, all of a sudden this faith rose up in me and I said God will take care of me, and my tree. A couple of days later lightning struck the tree about to fall on my tree, and cut off about 15 feet, so even if that tree fell it wouldn't reach the tree I planted. That was pretty incredible if you ask me.

How much chance is there of lightning hitting two trees right next to each other within a couple of days? As soon as I put my faith in God, He took care of my problem. Every time I get down and discouraged I think back on that incident and I'm encouraged. I know answers to prayer don't always come instantly, but they do come when our prayer is in accordance to the will of God. Keep praying and keep believing, God will do the rest.

During the next five years I was able to minister to many people whom I met at the park, the grocery store, in restaurants etc. I didn't get into any relationships or date anyone. All I wanted to do was reach out to people and share what God placed in my life. I will share some of those stories, and I hope and pray they will encourage you to share your faith.

One day I was walking around at work and this song popped in my head. This song was about a particular person named, which I won't mention to protect their identity. So the thought occurred to me to pray for this person who was related to me, which I had not seen in over a year. I asked a friend of mine to join me in prayer for her. I had no idea what was going on in her life. As we started praying for her, out of nowhere I started crying deep sobs, like my insides were about to fall out. I took it as something must really be wrong with her. I called her father and asked if there was something wrong with his daughter who was about 17 years old at the time. He was curious as to why I was asking him this. I told him he

## *Led by the Spirit*

wouldn't believe me if I told him. He said try me, so I told him what had happened. Of course, when I told him we were praying in tongues and about the crying bit, he didn't believe me or acted like he didn't. He told me it just happened to be her birthday that day, which I didn't know, however it later confirmed what was actually wrong. He told me nothing was wrong that he knew of. Then months later, I received a phone call from his sister who informed me his daughter was pregnant... and before I could get the words out of my mouth, she said "you remember when you called, it was nine months ago." I remembered because he had told me it was her birthday. Now remember this was nine months ago, when we had prayed for her, and this was around the time she became pregnant out of wedlock and possible suicidal as a result. I had also been told she had been suicidal a couple of times before, so I'm certain the prayer had something to do with that. She had the baby and married the baby's father. I'm sure she was probably afraid not knowing what to do. I believe that prayer helped her through this difficult part of her life. Thank God he loves us beyond our sin and weaknesses. His mercy endures forever.

Another time, I was at a nearby park I went to almost daily to talk to people and share the gospel. I met a young girl about 16 or 17 years old. I started telling her about Jesus, and she asked the question, "Why did God let my sister die?" My heart wanted to break. I told her I had no idea why God allowed her sister to die, but that I do know this; God knows more than we do, and whatever He allows has our best interest at heart. As I kept speaking to her, she seemed not to be paying very much attention. I spoke to her on a couple of other occasions, just seeing her in different places, never really planning to see her because I didn't know her well, actually, not at all or even where she lived. *But God knew...* and He placed her in my path. On most of the occasions I spoke to her, she had the same blank look on her face. One day she happened to show up at the restaurant where I worked. She walked up to me and said," Guess what happened? I got saved at my church and I told them all about you talking to me!" She said her church members said I was her angel, maybe one with a couple of broken wings. I had learned not to go by what I see. I didn't think she was listening, but it was obvious that she was. Praise God, to Him be the Glory.

## LESSON FIFTEEN
*Soul Winners*

What exactly is a soul winner? Is it a pastor, a prophet, evangelist? It's all of these, or at least it should be, but it's also me and you. Everyone who calls himself or herself a believer should be a soul winner. If you belong to the body of Christ, pull out your nets, your boat, whatever you will need to catch men and women, and bring them into the kingdom. The word of God says "he who wins souls is wise." (Proverbs 11:30) Are you wise? If not, why not? Let me guess, you're not good with words…well Moses tried that one, and the word of God says in Exodus 4:10, "and Moses said unto the Lord, O Lord I am not eloquent, neither heretofore , nor since thou hast spoken unto they servant, but I am slow of speech, and of a slow tongue, and the Lord said unto him, who hath made man's mouth or who maketh the dumb or deaf, or the seeing or the blind have not I the Lord? Now therefore go and I will be with thy mouth and teach thee what thou shalt say. In addition, he said O my Lord, I pray thee, by the hand of him whom thou wilt send, and the anger of the Lord was kindled against Moses and he said, is not Aaron the Levite thy brother? I know he can speak well and also he will cometh forth to meet, and when he seeth thee, he will be glad in his heart." You can try that one if you want to, but I wouldn't advise it, the last person's anger you want kindled against you is God. If we don't know what to say we can learn, God's a good teacher. Ok, one excuse down, what is next? "Oh, I am afraid there are a lot of crazy people in the world." Who's bigger God or crazy people? The word of God says "I have not given you the spirit of fear, but of power, love and a sound mind" (2 Timothy 1:7). So there you have it, you can help the crazy people to have a sound mind, and drive the devil crazy.

I know we have to use wisdom when talking to people, but if you open your life up to be used as a vessel, you will be surprised by the great things God can and will do through our feeble efforts. God's power changes people, not our efforts. Our efforts only open the door for the King of Glory to come into. Well, you say "I am too busy", well what business is more important than His business?

The word of God says "seek first his kingdom and his righteousness, and all these things will be added to you." I said that to a man I met on the street. He said, "Well I don't see no food on the table", and I said, "I don't see God first in your life either." We must believe and act first, and then we will see, not the other way around. I always tell people you will never know God unless you obey Him. You can read about Him… you can read about Him until you turn purple, but you will never know until you're a doer of the Word, not a hearer only. Bottom line, there is no other way, but to trust God. Three strikes, but I know you can't hit well, so I'll give you a few more swings. You say "well people will reject me, and make fun of me". Guess what, you're in good company, they made fun of Jesus too! So come join the team, you'll fit right in. The word of God says He was rejected and despised. If you want to share in His gain, we must share in His pain, besides you will receive greater rewards, not only for you, but for the person receiving salvation. One person you reach could reach many others. Only God knows the far-reaching effects of just one soul saved. It's like the domino effect, push one, they all go down. It also works in a negative way, when we don't reach out to people. That person that's not reached may harm a lot of peoples' lives. I know we can't talk to everyone, but we can talk to someone.

Well, you say I should preach by example… well I guess you know more than Jesus, or your example is better, and more effective than His. When Jesus met people he spoke to them. He didn't stand around like He was mute. In fact, He cast out that deaf and dumb spirit. Sometimes I do that to my children. I say, "Come out dumb spirit"…I'm only joking… *halfway* anyway. Sometimes I've had to do it to myself. I was always one to tell it like it is. The main reason we don't talk to people, which I believe this covers all other excuses, is that we don't love them. I know this sounds hard but sorry, it's true. If you saw someone about to fall in a fire, wouldn't you push them out of harm's way, even if you had to hurt them a little to do it. Sometimes the truth hurts, but in the long run its worth all the pain and more. So please let's drop all the excuses into the sea of forgetfulness, and get busy rescuing the hurting and the lost.

Once you begin, you will be glad you did, you will realize a lot of things. First, is that you can do this and second, how necessary and rewarding this is. You will also realize you have gifts you never knew existed. Sometimes, actually many times, I've been afraid and have been tempted with all those excuses we have, but I've found that when I just do it, regardless of fear or whatever the excuse, it's always a blessing for others and myself. I was helping an Asian lady with her car one day and I was wearing a pair of flip-flops and she told me I had beautiful feet. The first thing that came to my mind, was beautiful are the feet of them who spread the gospel. So let us get rid of our ugly feet and get some beautiful feet instead. Save a life it may be your own, God will bless you for your efforts.

# CHAPTER ELEVEN
## *Dreams and Broken Dreams*

One night I had this dream and in the dream I saw a book opened with writing on the pages, and at the top of the page were huge black letters, which said Philippi. The other things written were not legible. At the time I didn't know what that meant. I started asking questions and found out it was the city where Paul was preaching the gospel. I took this to mean I was to read the book of Philippians. This particular verse stood out, Philippians 2:3-4 which said, "Do nothing out of selfish ambition or vain conceit, but in humility consider others better than yourself". Each of you should look not only to your own interest, but also to the interest of others. To me that was a reminder to do everything with pure motives and also reaching out to others not considering just my own needs, but others first. I have done my best to help others from a pure heart. This should be the foundation of everything we do as believers.

Around the same time frame, within a month or so, I had two dreams or visions, which were related to one another. The first one, I saw a huge ball like the sun except it looked like diamonds or jewels, which were sparkling. I was looking up at this sun-like ball, and then it seemed as though someone through it at me. As it was coming towards me I covered my face and it shattered into broken pieces. Then a few days later, I had another dream or vision with those same jewels in the hair of a woman who was dressed like a prostitute or loose woman. I didn't know what it meant, but it troubled me in my spirit. Many years later I found out what I believe it meant. I'll share the meaning later.

# BROKEN PIECES

As I ministered more freely, God started teaching me much more about spiritual things, which I knew little about. One day I was driving my car and began praying in tongues, but this was different than I had ever experienced in my life and I have never experienced it again. I can't describe what came out of my mouth. It was a language, but with something else which I have no words to compare it to. If I had to guess it would be what the book of Corinthians describes as tongues of angels… but to be honest I can't say for sure. When Paul speaks in his writings, he talks about things he can't describe when he was caught up in the heavens. After I had prayed, the thought came to me to sell everything and follow him. I sold all my belongings and moved to San Diego, California. I believed I got out of God's timing. I stayed there only about a month. While I was there I just ministered to people I met on the streets. I will share with you a few of these whom I was able to minister to.

As I was praying one day, this woman's name kept coming up in my mind. I didn't know anyone in California. I walked around for two days looking for this woman, but I spoke to no one. Then I saw this lady sitting on the curb outside a restaurant, so I struck up a conversation with her. I asked her what her name was, but she would not tell me. I said "that's fine I don't really need to know your name." Then she told me her boyfriend would soon be coming back and he probably wouldn't like me talking to her. I said "don't worry God will take care of that for me. I just want to share the gospel with you." The boyfriend never showed up and I asked her if her name would happen to be Brenda. Her eyes got about as big as a plate. She said, "Yes, how did you know my name?" I told her God put it on my heart, she was all ears then. She asked me what God wanted her to know. I said "for one thing, not to live with your boyfriend, when you are not married." She told me she was thinking about going back home to New York. I shared God's love with her, I prayed with her, gave her twenty dollars and a Bible, and went on my way. I never saw her again. That has been the case with most of the people I've come in contact with, that God has sent me to. This I believe is the reason I was born to encourage the hurting and weak.

## *Dreams and Broken Dreams*

On another occasion I met another young woman and tried to share the gospel with her, but she told me she was in a hurry and she didn't have time. Two days later I saw the same young woman again at a hamburger joint. As I was talking with her she told me there was light shining from my eyes. I know it sounds crazy, but I'm only telling you what she said. I didn't see or feel anything, but she did. Whatever it was that she saw caught her attention, and she was now ready to listen. I prayed for her and I never saw her again.

I started talking to another man about Jesus and I could sense the Spirit of God very strongly. The man just started shouting, "I can see Jesus in you" over and over again. I don't know exactly what he saw, but from his reaction I know he saw or sensed Jesus in a very powerful way.

I was at this motel one day, and I met this lady sitting outside. I started a conversation with her and asked her what she did for a living. She just told me straight out, with no hesitation, "I am a prostitute". I told her she should get out of that life. I asked, "Aren't you empty on the inside?" She said she was, but she saw no other way to make a living. She told me she was going out that night to make some money, and asked if I would hold this duffle bag for her until she got back. I told her I would, but then after she left I started thinking, what if she has some dope in that bag? So, I decided to peak in the bag… it was only makeup, and things like that. I prayed for her that night, and as I was praying I had a strong sense like I didn't want anyone to touch me. I thought it probably was what she felt like while doing the things she was doing for money. She never returned for her things, I can only hope and pray nothing really bad happened to her. I can only say God reached out to her. If you're in this type of life I beg you to get out, God will help you start over.

A couple of days before I was about to leave for another city, I was at the front desk of the motel asking for directions. This young lady about 19 or 20, came in and started yelling at me, asking who I was and why was I asking all of these questions. I

# BROKEN PIECES

didn't know her and never seen her before. Then later that night, I was walking in the parking lot of the motel praying for the girl who yelled at me earlier. Suddenly, she drives up next to me and stopped. She told me she was sorry for the way she acted. But then she said one of the craziest things I ever heard… and she was dead serious. She told me she was a love goddess. I told her "no you're not; you have a demon spirit in you." I shared my testimony with her. She listened and the next day, just as I had finished praying for about 3 or 4 hours, I was walking out of the motel room and she pulled up outside my door. I gave her a book about giving thanks in every situation, prayed for her and then left. God wants to help you no matter where you have been or what type of bondage you are in. He wants to set you free. As I started running out of money, I got discouraged. I was at an apartment complex and this little girl walked up to me while I was sitting out front by myself. I don't know where she came from or why she was alone, because she was only about 5 or 6 years old. She walked up to me and handed me a little yellow flower and walked off. It really touched my heart. God really knows how to comfort us when we are hurting. Give Him your hurts and fears, no one else can help you and no one else cares more than God. After this I decided to return to Georgia. I felt defeated and was very disillusioned.

## LESSON SIXTEEN
### *The Silence of God*

What comes to mind when you read these words? Most people think God is angry when He is silent: sometimes this is true, but many times it is not. If God has spoken to you to do something or convicted you of some specific area of your life and you haven't responded…. your Father is saying *"mums the word"*, so don't be surprised. Why should God continue to speak to you when you haven't obeyed the first order He has given you!? He is wasting His breath; God does not like to waste His time. Would you give your son a $100 more after he has wasted the first $100? God is a good steward over everything he does. He doesn't have time to waste.

## *Dreams and Broken Dreams*

This used to really bother me that God would not press people once He spoke. God is not like the parent who gives three times and then says, "I am telling you and I am not going to tell you again"--- and then does nothing. When the rich man turned and walked away after Jesus told him to go and sell all his possessions, give it to the poor and come follow him. Jesus didn't say to him, "you don't understand" and continue to plead with him. Jesus allowed him to walk away. The Holy Spirit is a gentleman, He doesn't force us, once we make a choice though, we don't have a choice of the consequences that follow, This is crucial because sometimes the results can change the destiny of your life and even where you spend eternity. Wow, that is something to think about!

One reason God doesn't keep speaking is because God already knows your heart. We're the ones in the dark, not God. He knows the beginning from the end. Another reason is God wants us to serve Him freely because we love Him not because we are being pestered to death from guilt and condemnation or any other reason than you love Him. Do you want your children, wife, husband, friends to help you out of a sense of guilt or being forced or because they genuinely love you? How would you like it if your wife to be, had her father holding a shotgun to your back forcing you to marry old ugly Leah, kind of like Jacob was tricked into marrying. Jacob was tricked into marrying someone he had no affection for in order to get what he really desired, which was Rachel. Some people don't really care why they get your help as long as they get what they want. What an empty way to live. When we want something for any other reason than love we want it too much and that my friend, is idolatry.

Back to the point, to which I was speaking about God's silence. Another reason for God's silence is that it causes us to search our hearts. As long as we have the things we want, most people don't even think about their motives. When God withholds something from us, we begin looking for reasons. There should be a balance in this area. Some people always think something is wrong with them; others are the exact opposite, they think they could not have possibly done anything wrong or it's always someone else's fault. We should search our hearts, better yet, ask God to search our hearts, but don't drive yourself to the brink of insanity trying to figure out what's wrong.

I helped a young lady for quite a while and the first thing came to her mind when she couldn't get in touch with me was that I was just like everyone else. In this case, that meant I didn't keep my word, which wasn't true. Most people believe this because they never see it lived out in many people's lives. We all believe things like this because most people don't keep their word. Some people don't believe because they judge by their own unfaithfulness, also believing that everyone is like them. We can always be sure this is not the case with our heavenly Father. He is always faithful even when we are unfaithful. But when you are going through one of these periods where God is silent, it is very difficult especially if you are a new believer or you had many people especially those in authority, parent, pastors, police, etc., disappoint you or abuse their authority. The best thing we can do during one of these times is to mediate on God's faithfulness and His word and not allow Satan to bombard our minds with lies. For example, Satan will have you to think that God is not with you anymore, you are no good, or that there is not even a God…..In fact; God is love. If you don't know of any way that you have disobeyed God, just continue to do the things you know that are pleasing to God and be at Peace! Sometimes it's not because we are doing something sinful but we may be headed in the wrong direction as far as God's will is concerned. We can't hear God if we are always talking. I've talked to some people who you have to wait in a runner's stance, waiting for them to shut that big trap before you can get one word in… know anyone like that? Maybe it's you. No wonder God seems silent; we wouldn't hear Him anyway because we are talking so much we drown out the voice of God. We as people, have a limitation… that is *not* the case with God, with Him all things are possible. If God is silent, there is just cause, but not because of unfaithfulness on God's part or because of His anger, unless of course you are living in willful disobedience., Sometimes we don't hear from God because it's not the right time. In Ecclesiastics, the word says there is a time to speak and a time to be silent. If I want you to go and do something a year from

## *Dreams and Broken Dreams*

now, I don't need to tell you today. We know that most people don't prepare like they should, thinking they have plenty of time. They procrastinate until the last possible moment. You know what I'm talking about, that is why your house looks like a flea market open for business. Your husband or wife has been telling you for God only knows how long to clean that mess up--- *yes*, I know you. The bottom-line is whenever God is silent; know He has your best interest at heart. I know it uncomfortable, but push through it; it was uncomfortable on the cross, but for love's sake and ours, Jesus stayed until it was finished. Thanks be to God!

# CHAPTER TWELVE
*Bold Steps of Faith*

  Living back in Georgia, I got a job waiting tables at a Ryan's restaurant. I really liked this job because I like working with people and it gave me many opportunities to share Christ. There were three other Christians working there who shared my enthusiasm of faith. We encouraged one another and had a lot of fun. We prayed together many times. This was one of the best jobs I had, not because of money, I didn't make that much. I was doing what I loved and that was being around people sharing God's love. One day as I was working there were two ladies sitting in the section that I was responsible to wait on. They were no different from any other two women. I had no intention of talking to them about God, but as I walked up to the table, somehow I just knew they were gay. I told God "Ok what you want me to do about it?" He said "tell them to give up that lifestyle." I said "no way… I am not going to do it." But it kept bothering me to say something. So, I said alright God if I lose my job or they get up and slap me, whatever… I'll obey you. One of the ladies got up and walked over to the salad bar, so I decided to approach just the one lady. I walked up to her and said "the Spirit of God told me to tell you to give up that gay lifestyle." She looked at me like I was insane. Then she asked, "Are you trying to say I am gay?" I said nothing. Then she said, "Well I am not." I said "Praise God" and walked off. I felt like a complete idiot. I was thinking to myself either that wasn't God or she lied. About 5 minutes later, she walked up to me and asked if she could speak to me. I said, "Sure, I'll be there in a minute." Then she told me the truth. She said, "I couldn't leave you over there and not tell you that you are right." She told me she didn't even believe in God. The other lady joined her and told me at one time she was a Christian but fell into that lifestyle and God had been convicting her of this. She also told me if I had spoken to her any other way than kind and loving, even though I was right, she wouldn't have listened. She also told me later that same night she had a dream she was going up a hill and falling down and she woke up in fear. Then she said God spoke to her and told her "you fear everything but me." She said she knew she had to change. She repented and came back to the Lord. She came to church with me for a while then started attending a different church. I lost contact with her for years but recently, which was about 12 years later, I saw her again at Wal-Mart. She told me she was still serving God and she was happy. I am glad that I obeyed God and was a part of someone's life being changed for God's glory. Sometimes it seems scary to step out on faith… but it was worth it and more.

On another occasion, I stopped by the church I was accustomed to going at this time of my life to have some quiet time of prayer before going home from work. I met two ladies from Florida, (I'll call them Betty and Suzie, not their real names). They were in town to visit the Monastery of the Holy Spirit. Betty and Suzie decided to stop by the church where I was spending my quiet time of prayer. As I was leaving, I met Betty and Suzie in the parking lot. Betty asked me to pray for Suzie who was experiencing some demonic manifestations. They had just come from the Monastery where some of the demonic spirits started manifested themselves. Betty was pretty nervous and afraid to go back to Florida with Suzie in this condition. Betty told me Suzie had commanded the Priest to bow down before her, and when the Priest would not comply Suzie grabbed the Priest by the hand and bent his fingers back. Betty told me Suzie also started barking like a dog. Pretty freaky if you ask me!

The Priest threatened to call the police on Suzie if she wouldn't leave the Monastery. That's when they decided to stop by the church I was at to get some help for Suzie. Betty told me what was going on and asked if I would pray with her for Suzie. Betty and I prayed in tongues for quite some time until Suzie was back in her right mind. As the Spirit of prayer intensified, Betty and I broke out in laughter. I also experienced this laughter during prayer on other occasions. I believe it's a sign of victory in prayer. God's word says, He laughs at His enemies (Psalms 2:4, 37:13, 59:8).

## LESSON SEVENTEEN
*Fear of the Lord*

This is something that will deliver you from many troubles but it is also very misunderstood by most people, even people who belong to a church. I was speaking to a young lady one time, about this subject. She told me you're not supposed to be afraid of God, and in a sense, there is some truth to this, but in another falsehood. I quoted Proverbs 1:7. "The fear of God is the beginning of knowledge, but fools despise wisdom and instruction." I had my Bible with me and she just opened it at random and turned to this exact scripture. She believed in some kind of new age cult. I think it shook her a little, as it should have. I'm not saying we should go around tormented with fear, but we should have great respect and reverence for God and His word. I hear so many people who say how His blood covers us, but they are really acting as if we can pretty much sin at will. This is why you see so many people's faith shipwrecked. They have no real fear of God. Whatever God says, He means and He is not just trying to carry on a good conversation, or give you an opinion. A lot of people, because they are not judged immediately, think they got away with something. This is far from the truth because whatever a man sows, so shall he reap. God is not mocked, it says you shall, not might---the only thing is *when*. God is merciful, and gives us time to repent because He knows we are made of dust. You know the only thing dust can do is make a mess. Haven't we made a huge mess of our lives? I have, but I have given my mess to the only one who can fix it and the only one who really cares.

So if you're one of those people (I do not want to leave anyone out) who thinks he or she got away with something, I've got a message for you… you should be more concerned if God doesn't correct you than you should if He does correct you. I am not trying to make you feel like God's just waiting to hammer you, or strike you dead, only that God is not playing when it comes to sin. If you are not disciplined (and everyone undergoes discipline), then you are illegitimate children and not true sons (Hebrews 12:8). The fact that he died a brutal death on the cross ought to show us just how serious sin is, not to mention it breaks the heart of God. In 2 Corinthians 7:1, it says "Therefore having these promises, beloved let us cleanse ourselves from all filthiness of the flesh and spirit, perfect holiness in the fear of God." Is that our goal, to cleanse ourselves or to get away with as much sin as possible, and quote a scripture to justify our sin? Like we are saved by grace not works, lest any man should boast? That's all wrong; God does not save us in our sin, but from our sin. The true grace of God causes us to live holy. He came to deliver us from sin, and set us free from it. The reason we continue to live in our sin is because we have no real fear of God.

Philippians 2:12 says "Therefore, my beloved as you have always obeyed, not as in my presence only, but now much more in my absence, work out your own salvation with fear and trembling." Do you only do what's right when someone is watching you or when you think you will get caught? We do not realize it, but we have more fear of man than God. Man can't help you; he can't even help himself, so how is he going to help you? You are on camera 24/7; God always sees us… we can't hide, so do not waste your time trying, just obey God from the heart.

There is also another side of God, which not many want to talk about. There is also a severe side of God, for instance, take the story in Acts 5, about Ananias and Sapphire. They had property, which was clearly their possession, but they wanted to make themselves look good to the church, instead of being obedient before God. They lied about giving and what was the result? Well you know they both ended up in the grave, yet we think we can just do anything with no consequences at all. God's word says He will not always strive with man. If you're determined to live in sin, that is your choice, but it will be to your own destruction. So please friends, get your heart right before God, and let the fear of the Lord protect, and keep you…if you play, you pay. Do not play with God.

Someone once asked me why I always hesitate when asked a question. Do we always just speak without any thought as to what we say? Remember we will be held accountable for every word we speak, and that's why I hesitate before I speak. I want to make sure what I say is right, and also say it at the right time, and in the right spirit. Our words to some degree affect people's lives for eternity. We should be careful what we say. The word of God says "where there are many words, sin is not lacking."(Proverbs 10:19) So please let our words be few and far between, and be a light to others, not a stumbling block. May the fear of God remain in our hearts.

# LESSON EIGHTEEN
## Sanctification

This I believe is the process, which God takes us through to rid us of our impurities. This I think is a lifelong process. There are always deeper levels of faith and virtue, which we are able through the manifold grace of God, to achieve. That by the way is the only way to achieve it. Not all the self-help books in the world will help to achieve one ounce of real virtue or faith. God has to work these things in our hearts by painful deaths to self. Last time I checked, self does not want to die, not even a little bit. Before God can use a vessel, He has to clean it. One time I was drinking coffee at a restaurant and I noticed my cup was dirty. I said to myself who wants to drink out of a dirty cup, no one. God spoke to me through that. He told me neither does He wants to pour himself out of a dirty cup… I got it. This is the Spirit of God, He will except nothing defiled. This is the part of Christianity no one likes. Everyone likes the joy, peace, miracles etc. No one likes to die, but without death to self, none of these other things will come about. We say God help me be patient, then one of our coworkers or neighbors does something we do not like and we want to choke the life out of them. Has anyone prayed for this gift of the Holy Spirit lately? For long suffering? I did not think so, but how can we practice virtue if we do not have the opposite of it coming against us? Most people don't see it that way. In order to practice virtue, we must perfect the skill of being able to respond in unfavorable conditions that are used as incentives.

How can you love your enemies if you do not have any? I am not saying you should go out making enemies or looking for them, but if you're truly pursuing to live like Christ, there will be no shortage of them. This I can promise you. There are many things in our hearts we do not even realize are there, but God knows it is there. He allows circumstances in our lives to reveal them to us. Peter made his bold confession how he would die for Christ, and I'm sure he was sincere when he made the statement. How greatly did he err! I've made similar statements not realizing how much weakness, and sin was deep in my heart. Most people do not know because they are not looking at their own life, they are looking at all your faults, completely blind to their own. Some people do not know because they have never really been put to the test. I heard one man say he wanted to suffer like Jesus. I thought to myself when he said that, (a) he's very foolish, (b) he does not know what he is talking about, and (c) if he really suffered like Jesus he would be crying like a two year old for mercy. This is what I call the A, B, and C's of insanity. He may have meant well, but completely blind to what he was saying. When people asked the question, do you want to be like Jesus, most people would say yes, but do we really? He was a man of sorrows, filled with grief; we want the glory but not the suffering. Jesus said "unless you suffer with me, neither will you glory with Him." Romans 8:17?

Everyone wants a great body, but no one wants to exercise. Sorry but the fat will get fatter and the skinny, skinnier if we do not exercise. If everyone is kind to you, how do you know if you have a bad temper? You do not. You only think you do, so God has to let you meet a few knuckleheads to build your muscles. Maybe you're someone else's knucklehead. It seems like God is your enemy sometime and when we are going against Him, we are, in a sense like an enemy of God. The aspect that He hates is our sin, it is not us He hates, but our sinful attitude. So when you decide to serve God get out your exercise shoes, because God is going to wear them out, until we get in shape. Do not forget God loves us and wants us lean and clean.

# CHAPTER THIRTEEN
## *Blinded by Sin*

About a year after I returned from California I started getting very discouraged and that is when Satan really turned up the heat. He was out to destroy my life and ministry. One day while I was out at the park witnessing to people, I met a lady who had just recently moved to Georgia from Colorado. I reached out to her as I had done many times before. She had recently been legally separated from her husband. She was very troubled about many things and I tried to help by being a good listener and I did my best to encourage her... but she wanted more than a casual relationship. I didn't believe God wanted me in a relationship at this time, especially since she was still legally married. She could see that I really cared about her and that I was not out to hurt her in any way. I don't think anyone had ever shown a true concern for her without wanting something in return. I believe she began to have feelings for me. I also felt I was getting too involved with her and it was taking me away from what God called me to do. This was uncomfortable, so I wrote her a letter informing her I would not be able to spend time with her any more. She was upset and I believe she felt like she wasn't going to lose the one person who treated her like a human being, so she had one of her friends from church to call me and ask me to continue to be a part of her life as a friend. God already told me to end this relationship, but I allowed my feelings of not wanting to hurt her and my own need to be wanted, overpower my obedience to God. This was one of the biggest mistakes of my life.

I continued spending time with her, allowing my feelings to grow stronger, and six months later I ended up in a sinful relationship with her which devastated my spiritual life. I began getting my comfort from her instead of God. My life turned into a nightmare. Satan used her to destroy my life and ministry. She filled something in me I had always wanted. She loved me like no one else had ever done before for a season, but then like the word of God says in Proverbs 5:4, "it turned to bitterness." Anything done out of disobedience to God will not stand for long and it will fail! One day her ex-husband called her on the phone, blaming all his problems on her and then blew his brains out over the phone. He had threatened to commit suicide many times before, but this time he went through with it. After that she was never the same and our relationship broke into pieces along with my life and my relationship with GOD. I had no peace because I knew I should have never been in a relationship with her in the first place. One day I told God I couldn't leave the relationship even if I wanted to, so I asked God to take care of that for me… because deep in my heart, I still wanted to do the right thing, and deep in my heart I knew it was not His will. No sooner than I asked God for help, all of a sudden she decided to move back to Kansas City, Missouri, where she grew up.

God answered my prayer but not the way I wanted exactly. You see my feelings were still very strong and I still did not want to let go even though I knew it was the right thing to do. One minute I accepted it and the next I didn't. She stopped taking my calls and I was very hurt. I even became angry with her and wondered how she could do this to me when I gave up everything, even my relationship with God, to be with her. I believe God answered and said, "It's the same way you turned away from me after I shed my blood for you." Even with that revelation, I still struggled to forgive her.

For the next year I could hardly get out of bed. I was so devastated though I had asked God to help. I had never loved anyone as much as I loved this woman and now I had a huge hole in my heart. I remember becoming real angry because she left and hurt me so much that I couldn't stand the pain. I was at work one day and I was drained mentally, spiritually and physically. I looked up and told God the reason I can't forgive her was because of my pride…and as soon as the words left my mouth, I immediately felt peace and strength. I hit the nail right on the head and from that time on, God enabled me to completely forgive her. If we can't forgive someone, you can be sure pride is the root cause. Pride makes us believe that we would never do such a thing that was done to us. Somehow we think we couldn't or wouldn't do such a horrible thing not realizing that the only reason we don't is only because of the grace and mercy of God. I hear people say "I know I'm really nothing without God" but deep in their hearts they don't really believe that and that's why they judge people so harshly. We blindly exalt ourselves and put down others. Pride says *"I am better than that"*…Humility says *"If not for the grace of God, there go I."*

# LESSON NINETEEN
## Disobedience

Disobedience simply means refusing to obey, to be insubordinate. (Merriam-Webster) Have you been disobedient? Sad to say I have many times and every time it has cost me. First of all, why do we disobey God? Have you ever really thought about that very deeply? One reason is we deceive ourselves thinking God is holding out on us. That somehow we know more than God or He really does not have our best interest at heart. We basically call God a liar. He promised to meet all of our needs according to His riches and glory. It's obvious we do not believe that or we would just obey His word. Another reason is we want more than we need, so we try to take what does not belong to us. We do not realize every time we disobey, the one we cheat the most is ourselves. Another reason is we want to take the credit for our decisions so we can pat ourselves on the back. We love to exalt ourselves so everyone will think we are such great people. We want the credit for what God has done for us. Disobedience is so deep in our nature we can't obey God even if we wanted to, which we do not. You may say that is ridiculous, I want to do the right thing. I'm just such a good person. The word of God says there is none good; there is none that does right, no not one… that includes you. It also says that He gives us the willingness to do what is right and that our righteousness is filthy rags in his sight. Are you starting to smell your rages yet, or must I continue? As long as we keep trying to exalt ourselves, by doing things on our own, you will keep falling flat on your face. Pride goes before destruction, a haughty spirit before a fall, Proverbs 16:18. That's exactly what happened to Satan.

God gave Satan great gifts, power and authority, but it just wasn't enough for old Satan. He wanted more, and not only that, he wanted all the glory. We, without God's spirit, are just like him. You know Satan's famous words are "I will do this, I will do that", and the worst was "I will be like the most high God." That is a big no-no. God does not play that. Then look what happened… before he got the words out of his mouth good, he went flying out of heaven like lightning. See, the Wright brothers thought they invented the first airplane, but they were wrong, God did. Whenever we notice that spirit of independence rise up, you can be sure you're on your way down. What happened when Eve disobeyed God? One simple act brought the whole universe into chaos. Therefore, whenever you begin to think of disobeying God, remember your whole world can go into chaos. It only takes a small hole to sink a huge ship. Have you ever had those gut feelings to do or not to do something? I have and every time I have, I paid the price if I didn't obey my spirit.

I am not trying to say we should live by our feelings, I know we have to live by the word of God, but when you know in your heart of hearts you are suppose to do something or not do something, whatever the case may be, and it does not go against the word of God, just do it. You will be blessed and the people around you will be also. To some degree, the entire world is affected, because we are one body. Do you think Eve thought for one minute that her one simple act could change the course of history? I find that most people do not think much before they make a decision. That is why this world is in the shape it is in. I read a story about a man who was in a car accident while drinking. The police officer was very upset with this man. The man drinking sarcastically said he would pay for all the damage no problem. Then the officer took the man to the other car and showed him the other driver had been killed, and asked "can you pay for that?"

The story went on to say the drunk driver went insane, lost his mind, and ended up in a mental institution. This was all because of one simple act of disobedience. I plead with you to think before you disobey; it could cost you everything, even eternity. Do not chance it. Could this man have been forgiven? Yes a thousand times yes, but there are still consequences for our actions. Whatever a man sows so shall he reap. God is not mocked. (Galatians 6:7) We never know when our next bad choice may be our last. So let's make them count, obey God even when it hurts…by the way that's another reason people don't obey God, because it cost you something to be obedient to God. It could be your job, a friendship, or even your life. Eleven out of twelve of the disciples were put to death for being obedient to Christ. Although He was a Son, He learned obedience from what He suffered (Hebrews 5:8). We will suffer for our obedience to Christ, but you'll always come out on top in the long run. I can't say it enough, may our great God have mercy on us!

# LESSON TWENTY
## Separation

This I notice not only in my life, but also to varying degrees in all people God calls to himself. The word of God says "come out from among them and be ye separate, sayeth the Lord, and touch not the unclean thing, and I will receive you and will be a Father unto you, and ye shall be my sons and daughters sayeth the Lord almighty." (2 Corinth. 6:17-18). This is very troubling to many people; it was definitely troubling to me, especially when you do not know the ways of God, or when you are young in the Lord. Ever feel like an odd ball, and wonder why the people around you start treating you like an outcast.

You start feeling the pain and rejection of not being like everyone else. When you are going through this period of life, it seems very dark and everyone is against you. Have you ever been there? Not a very fun time! Even though you are just as skilled or talented and sometimes even more so, somehow unseen hands seem to hold you back from certain people or places that you associate with. At the time you are going through this you cannot understand what is going on. Little by little, God is calling out to you to draw nearer to Him. God wants you for himself. He is drawing you away from the clutter and clamor of the world to be still. This seems like a nightmare at the time it is happening, but actually, it is a great blessing which God protected you from being entangled in many sore troubles.

Another type of separation is sometimes from family or the familiar. Removing these hindrances is a way God begins to teach us to trust him. Whatever God sees in His infinite wisdom, something or someone that we lean on or rely on the most, He will remove from our life. He takes a big swing of the bat and knocks it out from under us so He and He alone will be the only thing to keep us standing. Whatever you are trusting in besides God, He will remove from your life. Cry as loud as you want to, He will not hear it. He loves you too much. Other times, there may be things other people are doing (not necessarily bad things in themselves, television entertainment etc.) but you have no peace about being involved with. The reason is God wants to remove from your life all the things that hinder you from having a close walk with him. "Therefore, since we are surrounded by so great a crowd of witnesses, let us lay aside every weight, and the sin which doth so easily beset us, and let us run with patience the race that is set before us. (Hebrew 12:1). What are these weights? Well they could be many things, certain jobs, friends, travel, hobbies, and sports. I am not saying you cannot do some or all of these things, unless they hinder your walk with God. Just a little poison can kill you. Be aware of anything that will steal your affection from God. Remember what we are made of, dirt. It does not take much to make a big mud pie.

What did your mama do when you tracked your muddy shoes through her kitchen? Out comes the fly swatter and you are the fly.

God is no different. God does not want us dragging our muddy shoes through the people in our lives' kitchen either. The kitchen is where you eat. God does not want us feeding His sheep the bread of life on a dirty plate. Another side of separation is this, "Who shall separate us from the love of God, shall tribulation, or distress, or persecution, or famine, or nakedness, or pen or sword." (Romans 8:35). All of these ways Satan tries to separate us from God's love, but God said it is not going to happen, that is my version…The bad English translation.

# CHAPTER FOURTEEN
*Another Trip Around the Mountain*

As time went by, I still felt alone, empty and forgotten by God. I was still hurting and wounded. My relationship with God was very weak and I was at the point of giving up...and in a way I did give up. I had lost my direction and meaning for the purpose of my life. When you don't know your sense of purpose, you lose your ability or you lose your willingness to keep on the path God has for your life. I was still praying and doing my best to obey God, but I didn't have the strength and enthusiasm I once had serving God. In my weakened state, I failed to learn from my previous situation. I got into a relationship that I knew I wasn't supposed to be in. I wanted to obey God, but I just gave in to the flesh. Six months later I remarried. When God tells you no, he means it...but if you are determined to have your way, He will let you go your way. And it always leads to trouble and heartache. I married in 2002, but by 2004 she had left. She had been married three times before she married me. Like I said before, anything you do without God's peace and guidance, will not last! There were some things she told me about her previous marriages that did not seem to line up with God's word for her to remarry, but I ignored it and did it my way. I paid a heavy price for disobeying God's word. For her sake I will leave her marriages between her and God.

I never felt at peace because I knew I should have never married her. We got along pretty good, but her children and mine became a wedge between us...and I had no peace about our marriage. I asked God to help me and if she was not suppose to be in my life to take her out of my life. Soon after that prayer she left. It hurt, but I accepted it. Eventually I would also have to accept other negative situations as a result of the marriage. While we were together we had made an agreement that she could use one of my credit cards during that time. She accumulated about almost 12 thousand dollars in debt and after she left, she quit paying the bills. The credit card company was harassing me day and night. The bill eventually reached 16 thousand dollars with interest. At some point, I stopped by her house and asked if we could talk about it. She told me to call her later but when I tried to call her she would not answer the phone. I kept calling her but I realized she had no intentions of answering. I left her a message on her phone telling her what a hypocrite she was. I didn't threaten her in any way, nor was that my intentions. However, I only wanted her to do what she had agreed to do, which was pay her debt. Next thing I knew I was being arrested for harassing phone calls. I spent only one night in jail, but that wasn't the point. I wasn't the one who lied and refused to pay the debt. I agreed to pay the debt that I was responsible for. The judge asked me why I was calling her. I told him the truth that I wanted her to pay the bill she agreed to pay. He asked her if that was true, but she told him it was things we bought for the house, which wasn't true, or at best, half-truth. She had taken the things with her she had purchased. She went free for lying and I went to jail for telling the truth. She also had a restraining order against me. I couldn't contact her and she couldn't contact me. If you disobeyed this order, you would go to jail for one year. While I was in jail, at the time when I was hurting the most, I still didn't want to have her locked up. Going to jail was not the worse part; the worst part was feeling betrayed and also finding out the next day she had someone living with her. She says nothing happened but this man lived with her for about 3 months.

During the first 3 months after I had been arrested I struggled between forgiveness and bitterness. I was willing to forgive her but bitterness was trying to get the upper hand on me. Remember during this time we were not suppose to have any contact between us, nor through a third party. Well wouldn't you know I got the opportunity to pay her back in full! Her son started texting my son who was living with me at the time, which meant she violated the judges' order, which also meant I could have her arrested. I believed with all my heart she would be arrested if I turned her in, that may not have been the case, but that's what I believed. Being the forgiving man that I am, I put out a warrant for her arrest. I wanted her to feel the pain I went through to let her know how it felt to be locked up like an animal. Previously I did not want her to go to jail, but as time went on and the pain increased, I allowed bitterness to take root never realizing it until I had the opportunity to get even. Sometimes bitterness stays hidden until God allows things to happen to shine His light on the things we have hidden deep in our heart.

During the few days that had passed after I had the warrant for her arrest put out, my heart was screaming at me telling me I was not right. God reminded me of the story in the Bible when David was being chased by Saul and had the chance to kill him. David's men said "God delivered him into your hands, kill him"... but David wouldn't have any part of it. Everyone was telling me "nail her to the wall" with the warrant, I was tempted but I did not have peace about this on the inside and knew my motives were wrong, so I obeyed God and had the charges dropped. As soon as I did this my peace returned. No matter how much I was hurting inside, I couldn't go through with revenge. The only one you hurt with revenge is yourself and your relationship with God. I knew I had completely forgiven her. I was at home and remembered it was her birthday. I chose to pray for her and forgive her. I told God I didn't know why she chose to do the things she had done, but I forgive her. Then I decided to go to the supermarket to pick up a few things. I actually saw my ex-wife as she was leaving the supermarket that same day. She didn't see me, but as I saw her, I realized the bitterness was no longer there; in fact I felt compassion for her. God not only shows you when you're hearts wrong, He also shows you when your heart is right.

When the court date finally arrived I chose to plead guilty to the charges even though, it was never my intension to harass her, but to settle our differences. We both had mutual friends who I did not want to involve in the court proceedings, this was the main reason I plead guilty. I was given a thousand dollar fine, one year probation and six months of anger management which I also had to spend another six hundred dollars to attend. God sustained me through it all. To Him be the glory!

Earlier I mentioned about the dream I had, looking up at the huge ball that looked like diamonds being thrown at me as it burst into little pieces, covering my face. I believe it meant I was throwing away what God was doing in my life for the sinful relationships I had entered. It was also symbolic of how my life was BROKEN into PIECES by my disobedience. The BROKEN PIECES also symbolized my shattered life. Me hiding my face represented God's presence being hid from me. After that, I sought God as to why I couldn't sense His presence. I was lead to a scripture, which says "because of your covetousness I hid my face" (Isaiah 59:2, Micah 3:4, and Ezekiel 39:23). As I was writing this last statement, God opened my eyes to see that is exactly what I did in the dream, I hid my face.

# LESSON TWENTY ONE
## *Forgiveness*

Forgiveness is defined as an act of pardon, or to overlook an unpleasant act. (Merriam-Webster) When Jesus was on the cross, His words and more importantly His heart cried out "Father forgive them for they know not what they do". **Luke 23:34.** What about if they do know what they do? Did Jesus leave us a loophole that we do not have to forgive, wishful thinking? No, I believe they knew the act they were doing but did not recognize the motive of their heart, because when we disobey the word of God or the conviction of our heart we are automatically deceived. When we hear the word but do not obey, deception is the result.

How can we forgive the horrible things people have done? I've got good news and bad news. The bad news is you cannot forgive others in your natural strength; the good news is Jesus can forgive others through you if you open your heart. Paul said "not I but Christ that lives in me". This forgiveness is a gift from God.

## *Another Trip Around the Mountain*

Sometimes people do horrible things and cannot forgive themselves; or maybe they have done horrible things to you. If they have, you are the instrument God uses to say from your cross "Father, forgive them." Am I saying you are God, *not hardly*, but God imparts His nature to us so we can impart His nature to others. Therefore, people may never be able to forgive themselves unless they see it demonstrated through us. In fact, this is exactly what Jesus has done for us from the cross. Do for others what God has done for you through the power of the Spirit. We will never be able to forgive unless we admit we cannot, not only that, but admit we do not want to. It is God who gives us this willingness to forgive. It is not going to happen any other way. The reason we cannot or do not want to is because we are filled with pride. Yes, I said it. That is the only reason, bottom line. We see others as worst than ourselves, but the word of God says we are to look at others as better than ourselves. When we do not forgive, we are the wicked, unforgiving servant who wanted to choke the life out of someone after he was forgiven a debt he could not pay. Donald Trump or Bill Gates does not have enough money to pay a debt this large. Only the Bank of Heaven has enough. Am I insensitive to the people who have been greatly hurt? No way, I am one of them. It will break your heart to even hear of some of the things done to people. However, the bottom line is we must make this choice. When we open this door of forgiveness to others, God opens His door of forgiveness to us.

Not all the money, fame, and glory of the world can give us what God gives us when we forgive…His peace which is priceless. We cannot have the peace of God unless we have peace with God and as soon as we open this door to others, the Spirit of the living God will rush in and heal, cleanse and comfort our wounds. Do not let Satan rob you of this priceless gift. There is great power in forgiveness both for ourselves and the one we forgive. Forgiveness is a one-time choice. There is a process we go through depending on the severity of the wound; a scratch heals much faster than a shotgun blast.

Do yourself and others a favor, let it go. God will put

people in your life who understand, who have walked the path your walking. You are not alone; stay connected to the body of Christ, and let the healing flow. Jesus' wounds will heal us, and our wounds heal others when we connect to the head. Remember it is His forgiveness, not ours. We are only fortunate ones to let it pass through us to others. We serve a great merciful God. To Him be the glory forever and ever, Amen!

Let me explain a little more about what I said about our healing of others--- *no I am not coming up with some new doctrine.* I am only trying to say that when God heals us of our wounds; we can draw from the healing God has given us. We can identify with others because we have gone through a similar experience. They'll know we understand. That is why Jesus became a man to identify with us. I am trying to say in a roundabout way, the scripture that says God comforts us and we can thereby comfort others. We are His body; let Him manifest His healing and compassion through us. Amen! People can tell if you are all talk, and no walk. If I go to war, I want to go with someone I know has been through some battles. How can we tell others how to get there if we have never been there ourselves? Search your heart well, do not deceive yourself, you will poison your own soul if you don't forgive others, make the choice – forgive.

## LESSON TWENTY TWO
### *Restoration*

Restoration means to return to a former condition, position, etc., to make amends. (Merriam-Webster) The word of God is a story about restoration, bringing mankind back to its original condition and position. What was man's condition and position before he fell? One thing is, we had unbroken fellowship with God. To me this was the worst of all things that could have befallen man. To have this fellowship with God is something that cannot be measured in dollars and cents. When we gave up our fellowship, we lost our sense.

## *Another Trip Around the Mountain*

To be friends with God is priceless. A man I met once told me that in this life you will have many acquaintances but very few real friends. He hit that one right on the head. This is the greatest gift in life, especially friendship with God. When Jesus gave us the Holy Spirit, that same Spirit restored our fellowship with God. Doesn't life stink when you have no one to share it with? To not only share it with someone, but with someone who loves you more than you love yourself. I know it's hard to believe anyone could love you more than you love yourself, but it's true. God not only wants to forgive us, but restore what we have lost through sin. To lose something and then find it again is one of the greatest joys in life. "Or suppose a woman has ten silver coins and loses one. Doesn't she light a lamp, sweep the house and search carefully until she finds it? And when she finds it, she calls her friends and neighbors together and says, "Rejoice with me I have found my lost coin". In the same way, I tell you, there is rejoicing in the presence of angels of God over one sinner who repents." Luke 15:8-10.

Do you need something restored? If you are breathing, the answer is yes. We all want to be restored, but not all are willing to meet the conditions to be restored. I once heard it said, we all want to be saved, but not from our sin. We want God to restore us while continuing to live selfish, prideful lives. That is a real shame, and on top of that, it will never happen. Do you have children that trample on your direction and counsel and still expect you to give them everything to waste on riotous living? Have you ever seen a pig with a wedding dress? NO! The two do not go together; nor does restoration and sin belong together.

When the prodigal son returned, he also turned away from his sin, and God not only forgave him, but fully restored him. That is why they had a party. Whenever we are restored there is a party going on in our hearts. In addition, when you have lost something, especially when we know we are at fault completely, and it takes a longtime to get back what we have lost, we have a much greater awareness of how easily we can go astray and ruin our lives. We also have a much greater appreciation for the things and people in our lives.

# BROKEN PIECES

Sometimes it only takes one bad decision to destroy our family, or even our lives. More importantly than both of these, is our relationship with God. Have you destroyed your life, family or relationship with God? I have good news; God is in the restoring business. God doesn't take things from us; we give them up for our selfish desires. Sometimes things are lost that can't be restored, until we meet Jesus. If you have been unfortunate to lose something like that, please don't spend the rest of your life beating yourself up. It's pointless, learn from it, and spend the rest of your life helping others, not to make the same mistakes. Life is not over; make the most of your future by building others up.

God promises to make all things work to our good, for those who love Him and are called for his purposes. Who knows if you had not made a mistake that maybe you wouldn't have helped anyone to overcome their mistakes or realize your need for God. You can also help others with much more compassion when you have been down that road. You get to share in the restoration of someone else's life. One of the most fulfilling things you can do in your life is to help return things that were lost to someone who is frantically looking for the things they have lost. The word of God says there is great joy when just one sinner is restored back to God. We as believers get to share in that joy.

Another thing God restores to us is our position. You and I both know if we are offered a position, we must accept the position and also keep that position by being responsible. Of course, we cannot do this without the grace of God. God restores authority to us, but to benefit us, we ourselves must be submitted to God. To the degree we are submitted is to the same degree of authority we are able to delegate in the body of Christ. By this, I mean spiritual authority, not telling everyone what to do.

Too many people try to use the authority Christ gave us without submitting our lives to the Lord. You will end up like those who tried to cast out a demon without being submitted to Christ authority. They ran away with no clothes on. Whenever we use His authority without being submitted we will end up being stripped of everything. Therefore, if you want to truly have your authority restored, submit your life to His word, nothing else will do. I have got a math test for you, love and submission equal power. Stay submitted to God and you will see His power and restoration at work in your life. Thank you God!

# CHAPTER FIFTEEN
*Refreshing Others*

I would like to share couple of stories which I believe sums up the message of the gospel. In the book of James, it states that religion that is pure and undefiled, is to look after the orphans and the widows in their distress. My definition of an orphan is someone without parents or someone who does not have someone to take care of them. Without the presence of God in our life we all fit in that category. So we as believers must help those who don't know that God the Father has adopted them.

One night while I was working late I got off about 1:00 am, I felt in my spirit that there was someone God wanted me to speak to but I didn't know who this person was. I was riding around the place I lived and I saw this lady walking the street half dressed. I rolled down my window and asked her to come see me for a minute. I started witnessing to her and she asked, "You called me over here to talk about Jesus?" With a strong accent, she told me, "I know I am a sinner." Then she threw a bomb at me. She said, "Do you want to sin a little bit tonight?" I asked her why she would say something like that after I just got through telling her about Jesus. She got pretty bold and so I got even bolder. I said, "I know why you said that, because you have a spirit of lust attached to you...and you like it too!" "I sure do!", she replied. I said, "But you wouldn't like spending eternity in hell, which is where you could end up, if you do not repent!" All of the stupid left her at that time, but I realized she was not the person God wanted me to speak to.

I still had that knowing in my spirit that there was someone else God wanted me to talk to. There was a small church in the trailer park where I lived at this time. As I continued to drive around, I saw a car parked at this small church in the trailer park that I lived in. I pulled up and had no idea who it was and for all I knew it could have been a murderer… but it just so happen it was the lady who lived next door to me. The first thing out of her mouth was, "God must have sent you here." She was having trouble with her marriage. I was able to encourage her and then she told me something that I knew nothing about. She told me that one day I was home and my window was open and her husband heard me praying in tongues. I had the windows down not to be heard, but because it was a hundred degrees in the trailer where I lived. She said her husband over heard me as I was praying in tongues and he told her what I was doing was of the devil. Sound familiar? That same spirit accused Jesus of casting out devils by the power of devils. Satan still uses those same tactics he's been using for over two thousand years. But she herself knew, the devil wasn't in me, it was in him. She also told me this was the first time in her life she had ever seen her husband so afraid of anything. Apparently, while I was praying, he trembled in fear. She told me that day God had convicted him of cheating on her. This is one of the many benefits of praying in the Spirit language (tongues). To God be the glory! After I talked with her, God released me, and then I knew in my heart that she was who God wanted me to speak to.

I have one other story for those who take the works of God lightly. A lady at work asked me to pray for one of her friends. About a week later the person who she asked me to pray for began working with us. She was living a pretty rough life if you know what I mean, drugs, sex, the whole nine yards. I talked with her about Jesus. She told me she had once before given her life to Christ, but soon fell away. I encouraged her to renew her relationship with Christ. She listened to what I had to say but I don't know if she applied it to her life. I asked if I could pray for her and she agreed. Shortly after she quit working and moved on. I do not know if she continued to follow Christ or not, but I do know God had given her an opportunity to come back to Him. A month later her friend who had asked me to pray for her told me she had been struck by a car and killed. She was only twenty-one years old. I believed I was placed in her life to encourage her to come back to God. I pray you listen both to God's warnings and His encouragement. God has skillfully planned your life; let Him use the BROKEN PIECES to be a source of comfort to others. (Proverbs 11:25) says, "A generous man will prosper; he who refreshes others will himself be refreshed."

As the old nursery rhyme goes:

*"Humpty dumpty sat on a wall, Humpty dumpty had a great fall, all of the king's horses and all the kings' men couldn't put Humpty Dumpty back together again"! I have GOOD NEWS: GOD CAN!*

# LESSON TWENTY THREE
## Born Again

I just wanted to speak a little on this subject. I don't want to assume everyone who reads this is born again. There are many I believe, who go to church, read the Bible, pray etc., who have never been born again. We need to make sure, if we are not sure. The difference is life and death, darkness or light. Jesus said unless a man (woman) is born again you cannot enter into the kingdom of God. Following some rules or saying a little prayer and continuing to live the same life is a sure sign you probably are not born again. You must ask Jesus to forgive you of your sins and turn away completely from the old life of sin and self will. Then you must ask Jesus to come into your heart and give you the Holy Spirit. God's word promises when you do this, that His Spirit will bear witness to your spirit that Jesus is in the house…that is just my little two cents. When Jesus is in your heart, there is no way you will be able to live in sin and have any peace inside while at the same time, having no intention of changing your life. Jesus and Satan are complete opposites. One of them has got to leave, but you're the one who has to show him to the door, it's your choice. Jesus said if we have His Spirit we will live like He lives. This is not a one day process, but if it does not start, you're only fooling yourself. You will have new desires and new strength to do what you could not do before.  By His Spirit, we will die daily to the old self and live after the new man.  Does this mean you won't sin...? No, but you will have the desire and the ability not to sin.

If we could not sin, the word of God would not have said, if you do sin confess it and God will cleanse us from all unrighteousness.  We grieve the Spirit of God when we sin or follow our own agenda.  The word of God also says He gives his Holy Spirit to those who obey Him, Acts 5:32.  We must be willing to obey in all things, not just the things we like or that which appeals to us.  Jesus said, "These signs will follow those who believe, they will speak in unknown tongues, cast out evil spirits, lay hands on the sick, and they will recover." (Mark 16:17-18). If we do not have any signs of God's promise we should seek Him and find out why.  There should be a change in our lives.

If I was born into the family of a poor man, you could tell by what I possess.  If I were born into a rich family you could tell by how I dress, or what I drive--- in the same way if we are born into the family of God there should be a difference between us and the people who are not born again.  If there is no difference there is a real problem; do not move on until you figure it out.  Jesus said we should be known for our love towards one another.  I know some people will never acknowledge you have changed, but you will know.  Some people accused Jesus of being the devil, so do not be surprised if they do the same to you.  We have some shortcomings and weaknesses, but just continue to grow daily and glorify God with your heart, before long people will notice you are not the same person you use to be.

We should be going from glory to glory, not failure to failure.  God's Spirit will enable us to be more like Jesus as we grow.  You don't become a man in a day, and you won't be mature in your faith in a day either, but we should be growing in the right direction daily.  You should not be sucking on a pacifier when you are twenty.  I know some people who are *still* on the pacifier, in their faith, twenty years later.  This is a shame and I know that I personally should be much more mature in the faith than I am today.  If we are honest, we are all not where we should be. We have all fallen short of the Glory of God. Make sure we do not make camp in our shortcomings or beating ourselves up for not being where we should be. Get up and keep moving, there are many people who need you. The stronger you are, the better it will be for the body of Christ. If you are not born again, please don't wait until it's too late. Please join the family! You will be glad you did and so will the people around you. Glory be to God!

# LESSON TWENTY FOUR
## *Fulfillment*

Let me ask you a question; is what you're doing in your life fulfilling you on the inside? Let me guess, no it's not. More than likely, you're not doing what God called you to do, or you need to change your attitude about what you are doing. You can go through your day with the attitude most people have, *same old boring thing, just a different day.* Is this how you want to live your entire life? I do not think so; in fact, I know you do not. So why do people live like this even though they hate the way they are living? Well there are many reasons. One main reason is we do not start our day meeting with God. Then by lunchtime, we want to choke everyone we see. You can't have a good day if we don't spend it with the source of life flowing on the inside of us. You know that old song "I have a river of life flowing out of me,"…is that what is flowing out of us? If not it is no wonder we are miserable. We have to get filled up before we can pour something out. What most people pour out is their bitterness, hurt and disappointment. No one really wants to hear that, most likely, his or her life is already filled with that.

Am I saying we should never express our hurts, disappoints, etc., *no*, but make sure the person you're talking to is mature spiritually and has the Spirit of God so that they can encourage you, because if you just start talking to anybody, they can potentially make your life miserable with negativity or lead you down the wrong path. I heard it said: to open your heart to one in a thousand, that is because nine hundred and ninety-nine will stab you in the back with the knife you just handed them. Moreover, pour out your hurts to God! You can be sure He really cares and if you need someone to talk to, He will send the right person across your path.

I remember one time I was so discouraged; I was visiting my children in another state. I was at this park sitting and thinking; God was nowhere to be found. I saw this man walking toward me and he didn't look like a follower of Jesus; he had no shirt and a huge tattoo on his chest. I was thinking "I wonder what this guy wants." He walked up to me, handed me a track and said, "God loves you." I busted out crying. He told me that God put it on his heart that he needed to tell this to someone. I am so thankful when people are obedient to God because I really needed to hear that. This man also told me that he was out of jail on bond, as he was charged with killing someone. I do not remember the details, but this just goes to show that if you judge by how a person looks, instead of their heart, you will miss God. Can you imagine having all that on his heart, about all the trouble he was in, yet he was reaching out to someone else? This is where I think so many people miss it, we are so consumed with our own little mess, and we can't see all the people around us dying for someone to care. I believe with all my heart when you start reaching out to others not only will your own needs be met, but you will be fulfilled on the inside, the only place it really counts.

Therefore, wherever you are in life you can start right where you are… on your job, at the park, at the grocery store, there are always people looking for a hand and a heart, let it be yours. The word of God says whatever you do, do it with everything in you. What people really want to know is do you really care about them, not necessarily what can you do for them, because many people will do things for you, but they do not really care about you. Love is what changes people, nothing else. Search until you find what it is that fulfills you, because that is where you will find the center of God's will for your life. You can do many things that bring you pleasure, but pleasure does not always fulfill you. In fact, if you

## *Refreshing Others*

search for things just to bring you pleasure; you will find yourself in a ditch sooner or later. You must find what brings you that sense of knowing that this was the reason I was born into this world. If you stay in your own little world of "me, me and me", you will never know the true joy of life. If you find yourself not wanting to reach out to others, ask God to give you a heart that loves to serve. I can promise you won't be sorry, only sorry you didn't start years ago. It is better to give than to receive, so start giving.

# CHAPTER SIXTEEN
*New Beginnings*

About four years had passed when my second marriage had ended. I had been through several jobs. God had begun to put the BROKEN PIECES of my life back together. I continued to share God's grace and mercy and have had many struggles. God continued to heal the hurts in my life little by little.

It's now the year 2011, I woke up one Friday morning and as soon as I opened my eyes, before I could think a thought, God spoke to me and told me to write a book. I said to myself, God did you fall off of your throne? Who would listen to me and my BROKEN PIECES? I have been through two failed marriages and too many struggles to say the least. He said "Just Do It!" I told God OK if you really want me to tell my story, show me what to do. I had no idea where to start. The following week, I went to church as usual. We had a visiting pastor, John Bevere speaking at Victory World Church in Norcross, Georgia. He spoke about writing a book; I knew he had written several other books. I didn't think that was enough confirmation. I then received a phone call from a friend informing me we had a meeting on Saturday. I hadn't heard from him in 3 months. I told him that most likely, I couldn't make it because I had to be home to sign for a letter, which would come on Saturday. Well, the letter came in on Friday. Even though I would normally go to serve at a local Outreach and feed the homeless on that day, I felt I should go to this meeting.

I went to the meeting and got there a little late. There were only a couple of chairs that were not taken. I had met a lady the previous week at the local Outreach, feeding the homeless. I introduced myself and found out we attended the same church. I do not remember seeing her before then. I knew nothing about her and she knew nothing about me...but since I had met her the previous week, I sat next to her during the meeting. After the meeting was over the leaders of the meeting asked if anyone had any prayer request. I informed them I was out of work and told them I drove a forklift. After we prayed, the lady next to me told me she didn't believe that's what God wanted me to do with the rest of my life which confirmed what was already in my spirit. When she said that, I broke down and cried. She then told me she had started her own publishing company with one of her friends. I told her God has spoken to me about writing a book. She took my number and we met the following week. I had planned to meet her close to her home, but instead she asked if I could meet her at the Mall. I noticed people met at a place called Borders, which was a book store; it didn't dawn on me until after I decided to meet her there that we were meeting in a book store. This was another confirmation. I told her my story and she agreed that I should write this book. I was asked by her business partner if God had given me a name for this book. I told them I believed the title should be called "Broken Pieces." The meeting went well. On the way out, there was a table set up with coffee cups for sale on it. As we were walking out, the young lady who started the publishing company accidently or I should say by the providence of God knocked one of the cups off the table and BROKE it into PIECES. That finally confirmed it for me! I picked up the pieces of the cup and handed them to the young lady working there. She told me to put the BROKEN PIECES down and she would take care of it. As she said that to me, I felt the Lord speak to me, telling me to put down the BROKEN PIECES of my life and He would take care of it. This is my story.

## LESSON TWENTY FIVE
*Purpose*

Purpose is defined as an aim or a goal or intention. (Merriam-Webster) I would like to talk a little about the two sides of purpose. First and foremost, we not only have a purpose, we were created on purpose. When God created you, He specifically created you, yes *you*. Many people I have met think they're an accident, because their parents never planned them, or they were the product of a rape, etc. Nothing could be further from the truth. Do you think an all knowing, all wise God would leave your existence up to man? "Who were born, not of blood nor the will of the flesh nor of the will of man, but of God." (John 1:13) Anyone who knows the nature of man knows God would never allow that to happen. Long before anyone was born God had you signed, sealed and delivered. His word says your names were written on the palm of His hand. (Isaiah 49:16) We were sealed with the Holy Spirit and delivered with a great price? Your Father had you on His mind with a specific meaning for your life. In Isaiah 44:1-3 it says, "Yet now hear O' Jacob my servant and Israel whom I have chosen, thus saith the Lord that made thee, and formed thee from the womb, which will help thee; fear not O' Jacob my servant, and thou Jeshurun whom I have chosen, For I will pour upon him that is thirsty, and floods upon the dry ground. I will pour my Spirit upon thy seed, and my blessing upon thine offspring." So not only were you specifically chosen by God, he tells you not to be afraid, and also that He will pour out His Spirit on you and meet all of your needs.

If you are waiting for people to meet your needs, you're in for a long wait. That is not to say God won't use someone to meet a need in your life, because He often does use people, but not when we try to make people an end in themselves... that is idolatry. We must always go to God first, not when we can't find anyone else to help us. How would you as a parent feel, after giving your child everything, you were dead last of people to come to when they needed help or love and affection. Wouldn't that cut your heart out? Yet we do this to God on a continual basis and think He's alright with that. Come on people, we were born at night, but not *last* night. It's not that God needs you or can't live without you, but He chose you and He desires to express His love to us. We need Him, not the other way around. If you're a parent, make sure your children know they are loved and wanted. Many children will get what they believe they need from others, like love, money and affection--- what they feel they are not getting from their parents. Whether this is right or wrong, they will seek it.

Parents make sure your children know you appreciate all they do for you. We are all a child of someone, so no excuses please. Well I got off the subject a little, but didn't want to forget something so extremely important. In Psalm 139:17 it states, "How precious also are thy thoughts unto me, O God! How great is the sum of them." Do you feel precious to someone? There is nothing better in life or of greater value than this need we have to be precious (important) to someone. Many people sadly have ended their life or at least quit living with any purpose or meaning, because of this. First of all this is a mockery to God. Would you go purchase something with no intention of using it, or enjoying it? That would be pretty dumb wouldn't it? Yet we accuse God of being dumb. Not a good idea calling God dumb. Not only purchasing something, but something extremely expensive: the price he paid was the precious blood of His only begotten son. There is that word precious again… that's why we are so precious to God. Have you ever given a child a toy that cost you little or nothing, and you can't pry it away from them with a two by four? Like that child with that toy that you or I know may be worthless as far as value, but it's everything as far as that child is concerned. Nobody is going to take it away without losing a few fingers. It's the same with God. Others may think you're not valuable, but as far as God is concerned, nobody is going to take His precious toy from Him. In addition, if you dare try, you may lose more than fingers if you try and take any of His precious children from Him.

## New Beginnings

The other side of purpose is you were called for a purpose and God has something specific in mind. Many think they can just do any old thing and God is tickled pink... not quite. God has something He specifically created you for, something He had on His mind, not yours. Of course He will let you know what it is, but we must seek Him and obey Him to figure this out. This is why so few figure it out, because we are too lazy to seek Him. We want Him to send us a postcard in the mail with specific instructions. God called us to be followers, seekers, not couch potato Christians, waiting for our next meal and someone to clean the mess we have made. No, you have to seek God, worship and pray like there is no tomorrow, because you might not be here tomorrow.

I know all the wives will agree; you should just know what they want; you're supposed to figure it out. This reminds me of a shirt a woman had on. It said, "Men are idiots and I married their king." She should have thought a little bit before wearing that shirt. If he's the king what does that make her, queen idiot...? Just joking! It's really unfair to assume to know what someone wants unless we tell them. God is no different; He wants us to ask Him what is it that He would like for us to do with our lives. The more obedient we are to God's word the clearer His will becomes to us. Remember, His word is His will. This should be common sense but most don't realize this, they are looking for something amazing to boost their ego. God does use amazing ways to speak to us sometimes, but it's my belief that we should not seek them or try to dictate to God how He should speak to us. If we do, Satan will more than oblige us. Remember He is always trying to make us exalt ourselves, not God. I have personally never once tried to tell or ask God to speak to me the way I would have liked it. I believe it's very dangerous to do this. Once, a lady asked me if I know a prophet. I should have said, "Yes, Jesus!...but I held my peace. I told her no and advised her not to seek one. The reason people seek a prophet is because they want someone else to do all the praying while they do all the playing. So, if you sincerely want to know God's purpose for your life, seek God not man or prophets or signs and dreams, etc. Friends, I pray that God's purposes will be fulfilled in your life; it will be your greatest joy. Amen!

## LESSON TWENTY SIX
*Passion*

Passion is defined as an intense emotion. (Merriam-Webster) This, I think, is one of the things that is greatly lacking in the body of Christ. I know we are not supposed to live on emotion alone but also we should not live without emotion. I believe there should be a balance. The word "E"- motion. This thought occurred to me so do not look this up in your dictionary because it is an analogy. The "E" is for effort and motion working together fueled by the fire of God. Note in the meaning where it says intense desire… anything God does is intense. We as believers will never accomplish anything for the kingdom of God unless we have passion.

We must have passion when we pray. Most people pray like they are talking to someone they have never met or someone they do not like. God is a passionate lover- see the Songs of Solomon Chapter 4 which says, "Behold you are beautiful my love behold you are beautiful! Your eyes are doves behind your veil. Your hair is like a flock of goats, moving down the slopes of Gilead, your teeth are like a flock of shorn ewes that have come up from the washing, all of which bear twins, and not one among them is bereaved. Your lips are like a scarlet thread and your mouth is lovely, your cheeks are like halves of pomegranate behind your Biel; your neck is like the tower of David for an arsenal where on hang a thousand bucklers, all of them shields of warriors. Your two breasts are like two fawns, twins of a gazelle that feed along the lilies. Until the day breathes and the shadows flee…I will hide me to the mountains of myrrh and the hill of frankincense. You are all fair; my love there is no flaw in you. Come with me from Lebanon my bride."

What would happen if you spoke to your wife that way? She would think you either lost your mind *or* you really loved her. Let me tell you they would not need to sell Viagra anymore, because you would be ready. She would not be saying "not tonight honey, I have a headache." She would be saying "let us put the kids to bed early tonight." Let me tune it down a little… before you run home from work.

When we talk to people about God, we act like we are giving out their last will and testament. It's no wonder people do not want to serve God. We cannot serve God half-heartedly. God said be hot or cold. Do you want your wife to be a hot babe or a cold fish? I think I know your answer. Even when Jesus fixed fish for His disciples, He made it hot. Come on Church; pray that God gives us a passionate heart. How does God do it? Glad you asked! Let's talk about being consumed or having zeal. The word consumes means to make use of, to deplete, devour or destroy. (Merriam-Webster) Those are some strong words. The word of God states the Kingdom of God suffers violence and the violent take it by force.

The act of being consumed is the force behind our passion. Do we go after God with force or do we act like a woman I spoke with. I asked her if she prayed. She said yes, whenever she had a few spare minutes. I told her "so in other words you give God the crumbs that fall from the masters table." She saw herself after I gave her that Polaroid picture! In Songs of Solomon Chapter 3, God describes how we pursue Him and how God pursues us. "Upon my bed by night I sought him whom my soul loves, I sought Him but found him not. I called Him but he gave no answer. I will rise now and go about the city in the streets and in the squares. I will seek Him whom my soul loves but found Him not the watchman found me as they went about in the city. Have you seen Him whom my soul loves? Scarcely had I passed them when I found Him whom my soul loves I held Him and would not let Him go. Until I had brought him into my mother's house and into the chamber of her that conceived me, I adjure you O daughter of Jerusalem by the gazelles or the hinds of the field that you stir not nor awaken love until it please."

What would you think if you went home from work and your wife greets you with a big wet kiss and says "Glad to see you honey. I missed you today." Then she said, "…relax while I get you some dinner." *Then* after dinner she says …"relax, I will clean the dishes." *Then* after that, says "wait a minute while I take a shower to freshen up." *Then* she comes out smelling like the rose of Sharon. *Then* gives you a little massage, *then* she gives you a little kiss on your neck---! UH, O MY BABY IS READY!  KA BOOM…all you men say AMEN and AGAIN I SAY AMEN!

That is a little demonstration of how God wants us to be consumed with PASSION.  As we study the word of God and meditate on it, most important of all we need to OBEY it!  God draws us little by little until that spark turns into a forest fire.  We cannot make the fire; we can only put together the ingredients and make it possible to ignite, like putting a match next to a gas can but only God can strike the match.  So get out your match and gas, the Word and the Spirit.  Obedience will light the flame and keep it burning.  Spend time alone with God.  Invest your time with God; it will surely pay off big!

# CONCLUSION

Here, I would like to make a few final comments. First, I would like to say to all of the people I have failed or disappointed, especially to those who know me well, that I am truly sorry and I make no more excuses for my shortcomings and failures. However, I would not be able to identify with weaknesses and failures had I not struggled myself. In Hebrews Chapter 5 it states, "For every high priest that is selected from among men and is appointed to represent them in matters related to God that he may offer gifts and sacrifices for sins. He is able to deal gently with those who are ignorant and are going astray, since he himself is subject to weakness this is why he has to offer sacrifices for his own sins as well as the sins of the people." I know Jesus died once for all and paid the price for our sins. I am not trying to say I am offering sacrifices for sin, I am only trying to relay the message that, because I have struggled with weakness, sin and failure, it is much easier to look at people from the same level and I can pray more effectively because I know by experience their struggles and pain.

So instead of wasting your life beating yourself up, take the BROKEN PIECES of your life and give them to the only one who can put them back together again. As Jesus has shown mercy to you, show the love and mercy you've been shown, to others, especially those whom have hurt you the most. I pray that this book will encourage you to continue your journey to the other side where they will be no more tears, but unstoppable joy and full of glory.

www.ingramcontent.com/pod-product-compliance
Lightning Source LLC
Chambersburg PA
CBHW032127090426
42743CB00007B/503